What the reviewers are saying . . .

". . . as eloquent as it is provocative. It is well worth reading."—Franklin Sherman, *The Christian Century*

"William Stringfellow, an Episcopal lawyer and theologian, is one of the most vigorous Christian writers of our time. . . . The writing is vintage Stringfellow— fresh, tough, pungent, and provocative. . . . A book to read, ponder, and ask if in my church 'conscience is an expression of the identification of baptized people with the whole of humanity.' "—John A. Lapp, *Provident Book Finder*

"The author works with the reader in helping to form a biblical hope which both understands *and* transcends politics."—Raymond McCallister, Jr., *The Disciple*

"Stringfellow's gift to us is that he raises questions which are undeniably biblical and which, perhaps especially in the United States, receive pathetically little scrutiny."—Charles P. Lutz, *Book News Letter*

"The author, attorney and layman, once again has written a book worth reading by those concerned as to the proper role of the Christian church. Particularly it should be studied, and carefully, by that body's leaders. . . . Find a copy of this excellent publication and read Stringfellow's viewpoint for yourself."— Cecil B. Currey, *The Tampa Tribune-Times*

"The sense of transforming justice may redeem not only the book but the reader."—Richard F. Boeke, *The Churchman*

by the same author

as co-author, with Anthony Towne

WILLIAM STRINGFELLOW

Conscience & Obedience
THE POLITICS OF ROMANS 13 AND REVELATION 13 IN LIGHT OF THE SECOND COMING

Wipf & Stock
PUBLISHERS
Eugene, Oregon

Wipf and Stock Publishers
199 W 8th Ave, Suite 3
Eugene, OR 97401

Conscience & Obedience
The Politics of Romans 13 and Revelation 13 in Light of the Second Coming
By Stringfellow, William
Copyright©1977 by Stringfellow, William
ISBN: 1-59244-879-8
Publication date 6/8/2004
Previously published by Word Books, 1977

**for
post-americans**

Foreword to the 2004 Edition

The publication of these volumes, first in a reviving series of William Stringfellow's remarkable corpus, couldn't come at a more welcome moment. This, not only because the appearance roughly marks the twenty year anniversary of his death, March 2, 1985, but because their clear-eyed prescience will serve Christians and others in the current historical moment. These were important books when they were written, and may actually prove even more so now. As Karl Barth, the great German theologian, once quipped to an audience regarding Stringfellow, "You should listen to this man!" It is not too late to heed him.

Of his sixteen books, these three—*An Ethic for Christians and Other Aliens in a Strange Land, Conscience and Obedience,* and *Instead of Death*—comprise something of an ethics trilogy. Stringfellow himself regarded the first two in such a relationship (anticipating another unfinished at his death) and the latter serves well to suggest a sequence. In their present form these books were published within a term of four years (1973–1977), a tumultuous period in U.S. politics covering the end of the war in Southeast Asia, the collapse of the Nixon presidency under the weight of Watergate, the elaborate mythic ritualization of the Bicentennial celebration, and the emergence of what Stringfellow termed "technocratic totalitarianism."

Because his ethics are sacramental and incarnational, advocating discernment of the Word within the contestations of history, mentioning those events is not incidental. What remains so striking is that his uttered vision in that moment and from that vantage should peer so deeply and precisely into our own. These books fall open as to the present, unsealing the signs of our own times. Technocratic totalitarianism indeed.

Because he urges a biblical ethic which is rooted in vocation—thus implicating our lives, our biographies, and our identities in the Word of God—it is equally apropos to mention his own involvements in this period. Stringfellow was then living with his partner, Anthony Towne, on Block Island off the Atlantic coast, where he kept something of a monastic regimen and was active in town politics. Having recently survived life-threatening illness, he remained a permanent, if vigorous, invalid—managing throughout to travel, speak, and write with great authority. He was certainly the subject of government surveillance in these years, having recently been indicted for "harboring a fugitive," namely his friend, the anti-war priest and poet, Daniel Berrigan. In this same period, moreover, he himself had called for the impeachment of President Nixon, prior to Watergate and on the basis of war crimes. Meanwhile on the churchly front, he served as canonical counselor and defender of the first Episcopal women priests irregularly ordained.

Years prior he had been an international leader in the postwar ecumenical student movement, and in that connection first heard tell of the "principalities and powers" in the sober witness of those emerging from the confessional resistance movements of Europe. That theological insight was verified by his own experience in New York's East Harlem ghetto where, after graduation from Harvard Law School in 1956, he took up residence to practice and improvise street law. His neighbors spoke openly of the police, the mafia, the welfare bureaucracy, even the utility companies as though they represented the power of death—predatory creatures arrayed against the community. Stringfellow took the clue biblically. He ran with the book.

No theologian in the United States did more, though generally uncredited, to bring the biblical view of the "powers" back onto the map of hermeneutics and theological ethics. Each of these volumes, in different ways, reflects that effort. This includes naming the power of death as a living moral reality and recognizing it, in the era of the fall, as the very power behind the powers.

Each of them also variously bespeaks Stringfellow's concern for the Constantinian captivity of the church, and with it, side by side, the moral justification of the nation as divinely sanctioned. He beheld the theological elaborations of "America" as the justified, elected, and righteous empire to be a form of blasphemy. Yet if anything, in our own moment, empire has been more openly embraced than ever as a divinely authorized vocation, a presumption of historical sovereignty, a Manichean mission in the world of both global terror and corporate globalization. If for none but that reason alone, these pages light up our own moral landscape.

Conscience and Obedience treats ethics and eschatology as a single matter. It does so by setting side by side two New Testament texts notably in tension: Romans 13 and Revelation 13. In the process the biblical sparks fly upward, illuminating the present moment. There is no New Testament passage more consistently abused than the 13th chapter of Romans. It is seized upon by ruling authorities near and far to claim divine sanction for their own regime. To do so they separate it from the nonviolent resistance invited and provoked in chapter 12. And yet by treating the "powers that be" apart from his customary eschatological expectation which anticipates the dethroning, or destruction, or devastation of all political authority in the reign of Christ, Paul did indeed set down a passage which, read in isolation, is vulnerable to imperial hermeneutics. By reading it in the light of apocalypse, against the terrain walked by the raging Beast of Revelation 13, Stringfellow restores the eschatological alienation that marks Christian political ethics. This does not thereby resolve the tension, reducing ethics to some contrarian principle. The Lordship of Christ, in which that dethroning is named, is not a divine title in Stringfellow's reading but a human one. It identifies the restoration of dominion over the powers in the new humanity.

In a moment when empire is so fully embraced and thought to be divinely sanctioned—and, not incidentally, in which a virtual publishing industry has sprung up in the business of twisting the apocalyptic parables into a series of novels serving the present regime—this book couldn't be more timely. Add only the notice that its sober closing meditation, "A Homily on the Defeat of the Saints," is worth the price of the book.

It is to be expected that some will find these volumes somber, dark, and theologically gloomy. So be it. Such times are our own. They remain, nevertheless, the most hopeful books I have ever read. They name the militant activity of the Word of God, present and efficacious, in the darkest of historical circumstance. Stringfellow had the gift to look the beast in the eye and, in faith, neither flinch nor fail. The realism of his gaze is inseparable from true Christian hope. So much else is denial, wishdream, and hope gone cheap. May the reappearance of these volumes summon us simultaneously to the truth of our times and living of that hope.

Feast of All Saints 2004
Bill Wylie-Kellermann

contents

Preface

My sole intention in this book is to affirm a biblical hope which comprehends politics and which transcends politics.

That hope, insofar as it is yet given to me to speak of it, is specifically grounded in the New Testament, which exposes the transience of the politics of this world, but which forebears to renounce political involvement, and which believes the sovereignty of God during this passing age. Simultaneously, the biblical witness anticipates, with extraordinary eagerness, and with no less remarkable patience, the end of this world's politics, the perishing of this age, the judgment of the nations and principalities and all rulers, the next advent of Jesus Christ, openly and triumphantly, to vindicate his reign as Lord.

If my purpose appears audacious—more readily announced than accomplished—I admit it. That attribute, however, has not inhibited the attempt, which various events have assigned to me, of this book. On the contrary, the diligence required to be coherent about the political hope of biblical folk in the present time indicates the task is cogent.

I became persuaded of this while I was engaged in writing *An Ethic for Christians and Other Aliens in a Strange Land.* That effort treats the Babylon passages in The Revelation to John as parable of the fallenness of the nation—be it America or any other nation or similar principality. In Revelation the predatory character of the nation is so emphatic that, as I dwelt upon this rudimentary relationship of the nation or principality to the power of death, it finally convinced me that I would have, next, to deal bluntly with other parts of the New Testament witness which *prima facie* bespoke different views of the nation, theologically or empirically. Hence, acquaintance with *An Ethic for*

9

Christians and Other Aliens in a Strange Land is more or less presupposed here.

I have chosen to deal with two biblical passages which represent the tension, internal to the New Testament, pertinent to political authority: Romans 13 and Revelation 13. These are the most famous texts posing distinguishable, perhaps contradictory, attitudes toward the nation within the Bible. They are also, probably, the two most abused citations among any that might be named. Both passages are published in this volume in order to prompt those who read what I have written to have direct recourse to them.

The historical circumstances in which each of these parts of the New Testament were uttered are quite different, and account is taken of that fact in my own comprehension of Romans, on one hand, and Revelation, on the other. I am not one, however, inclined toward using the conditioning of history to explain away discrepancy or incongruity in the Bible. At the same time, I harbor no compulsion to neatly harmonize Scripture, as I have elsewhere often remarked. The whole notion that the Bible must be homogenized or rendered consistent is a common academic imposition upon the biblical literature but it ends often in an attempt to ideologize the Bible in a manner which denies the most elementary truth of the biblical witness, namely, that it bespeaks the dynamic and viable participation of the Word of God in the common events of this world. The militant character of the Word of God in history refutes any canon of mere consistency in the biblical witness. To read the Bible is to hear of and behold events in which the Word of God is concerned, attended by the particularity and, to human beings, the ambiguity of actual happenings. Any efforts to read the Bible as a treatise abstractly constructed or conformed usurps the genius of the Bible as testament of the Word of God active in history. If the biblical witness were internally strictly consonant, after the mode of ideology or philosophy, the mystery of revelation in this world would be abolished; revelation itself would be categorically precluded.

What is to be expected, instead of simplistic consistency,

in listening to the Bible, allowing for the vagaries and other limitations of human insight, is coherence: a basic integrity of the Word of God or the fidelity of the personality of God to his creation.

I do not mean to extol inconsistency. I am glad enough to find one text of the Bible which seems, to my mind, in obvious harmony with another passage, but I do mean to caution against making a rubric of consistency that violates the most essential characteristic of the biblical witness and which, usually, nourishes vanity in reading and using the Bible, and which, invariably, issues in manipulation, or oversight, or suppression of certain dimensions of the Bible.

This is how I come to the texts from ROMANS and REVELATION. If the two seem at odds—though variant historical situations are to be taken seriously, and while the partiality of a person's perception at a given moment has to be acknowledged—perchance it is because they *are* at odds. That, to me, becomes primarily significant as a clue to the vitality of the Word of God in the world. The revelation of the Word of God is, always, more manifold and more versatile than human comprehension. What I anticipate in the passages is not consistency so much as coherence. I can live and act as a biblical person without the former, but without the latter I cannot live.

So in the Bible and, here, in ROMANS and in REVELATION, I look for style, not stereotype, for precedent, not model, for parable, not proposition, for analogue, not aphorism, for paradox, not syllogism, for signs, not statutes. The encounter with the biblical witness is empirical, as distinguished from scholastic, and it is confessional, rather than literalistic; in either case, it, over and above any other consideration, involves the common reader in affirming the historicity of the Word of God throughout the present age, in the biblical era and imminently.

My esteem for the biblical witness and my approach to the Bible should be enough to disclose my skepticism about current efforts to construct political theology according to some ideological model. I refer, for one specific example, to attempts to articulate a pseudo-biblical rationale for classical Marxism, which have lately become prominent, oddly enough, simultaneously, in both some post-industrial societies of North America and Europe and in still pre-industrialized regions of Asia, Latin America, and Africa. It is persuasive of the ideological bankruptcy of the former that anyone would imagine that Marxism sponsors a social and economic analysis relevant to the conditions of advanced technology and the technocratic state; in the Third World, at least, the prevailing society retains a semblance to those conditions which originally occasioned Marxism, more than a century ago. Given the analytical naïveté of the revived interest in Marxism in a country like the United States, it may be that the phenomenon is mainly rhetorical, with classical Marxism supplying a convenient and ample lexicon with which to denounce the regime. Or, in addition, this belated attention to Marxist ideas may express the profound frustrations of people wrought in the decadence, and obsolescence, of American capitalism. Or, this may also be an aspect of the vogue of nostalgia that accompanies the endemic apprehension of Americans concerning the failure of the system. If that be true, it is quaint and pathetic since nostalgia signifies an inverted eschatology, as such the most fictionalized and forlorn hope of all. Meanwhile, even in sectors of the Third World where Marxism may remain analytically cogent, the attempt to theologize, in biblical terms, ideology is untenable. Even that most venerable identification and advocacy of the biblical witness for the dispossessed and oppressed of this age does not render the biblical people ideologically captivated. The effort to distinguish a biblical apologetic for Marxism is no different from those which have sought to theologize capitalism, colonialism, war, and profligate consumption. Whatever the subject ideology or policy, attempts such as these trivialize the Bible.

In other words, biblical politics *never* implies a particular, elaborated political theology, whether it be one echoing the status quo or one which aspires to overthrow and displace the status quo. The gospel is not ideology and, categorically, the gospel cannot be ideologized. Biblical politics always has a posture in tension and opposition to the prevalent system, and to any prospective or incipient status quo, and to the ideologies of either regime or revolution. Biblical politics are alienated from the politics of this age.

Let no one read into these remarks gratuitous comfort for simplistic and unresponsive answers to political issues of enormous complexity, such as all the nations suffer, after the manner, for instance, of those who incant the name of Jesus superstitiously. It is literally pagan, unbiblical, to so recite "Jesus is the answer". The Bible is more definitive, the biblical affirmation is "Jesus is Lord!" The Bible makes a political statement of the reign of Christ preempting all the rulers, and all pretenders to thrones and dominions, subjecting incumbents and revolutionaries, surpassing the doctrine and promises of the ideologies of this world.

Nor is there, here, furnished any pretext whatever for the neglect of the poor or the unliberated, or for abandonment of the biblical advocacy of the oppressed and the imprisoned. On the contrary, the exemplification of redeemed humanity in the Lordship of Jesus Christ in this age means a resilient and tireless witness to confound, rebuke and undo every regime, and every potential regime, unto that moment when humankind is accounted over the nations and principalities in the last judgment of the Word of God.

The approach to ROMANS 13 and REVELATION 13 here is confessional, that is to say, a living contact betwixt the Word of God exposed in the biblical texts and the same Word of God active now in the situation of the common reader so that the encounter in Bible study becomes, in itself, an event characteristically biblical. As such this book is not exegetical in a technical sense, though I do not imply that technical work on these passages is unimportant or that it is incompatible with a confessional style in Bible study, or that it can be ignored by laypersons. I am, rather, emphasizing that this book is primarily a pastoral endeavor. It seeks to literally encourage a biblical lifestyle in the politics of the age in—as the subtitle states—conscience and obedience in church and in nation while awaiting the promptness of the Lord.

Similarly, though the work is about politics, it is not a technical piece and does not enter the realm of political theory or employ the jargon of the discipline of political science. Such political terms as are mentioned are utilized in obvious connotations and not as words of art or of technical definition.

Perchance particular notice should be given to the usage in this book of the phrase *the Word of God*. I intend this to be understood as a name. Thereby I refer not only to the Bible as the Word of God, but, simultaneously, to the Word of God incarnate in Jesus Christ, and, also, to the Word of God militant in the life of the world as the Holy Spirit, and, further, to the Word of God inhering in the whole of creation.

To confront the issues of conscience and obedience in church and nation, in the time being, with reference to the testament in ROMANS and in REVELATION, involves treating ethics and eschatology simultaneously instead of as distinct or separated categories. I believe that it is the disability within Christendom to comprehend ethics and eschatology as subjects encompassing one another which chiefly accounts for the impairment of the political discernment of the church, in America as elsewhere, in the present as previously. If I deal in the same thought with ethics and eschatology, however, it is not because I indulge either inflated ethics or realized eschatology. (A popular current temptation is somewhat different—that is, the displacement of ethics by a realized apocalypticism rather than fantasizing eschatology.)

I just affirm in this book the elementary link between ethics and eschatology, which is that the topic of both is *hope in its relationship to judgment*. If I comprehend ethics as eschatological anticipation or as herald to the judgment of the Word of God in history, and if I foresee the eschaton as the consummate ethical event pertinent to the politics of this age, I am saying that hope—hope *now* for human life—hope *now* for nations and principalities—hope *now* for the whole of creation—means the imminence of judgment. That is the pervasive biblical theme; it is what I hear in the passages at hand in ROMANS and REVELATION. In biblical faith, ethics and eschatology coincide because the common history of the world is beheld as the redemptive history of this world.

This may explain why I find the familiar reputations of ROMANS 13 and REVELATION 13 curious. The Book of Revelation, including this citation, is often ignored or suppressed because it is reputed to be such a heavy eschatological utterance that it supposedly has little contemporary significance. The first seven verses of ROMANS 13 are commonly exempted from context and commended as prudential guidance here and now without particular cognizance of the impending distress to this world of the eschatological reality. The more I have lived with these two texts, the more I perceive them oppositely. ROMANS 13:1-7 bears an explicit eschatological context; REVELATION 13 focuses upon the politics of the passing age, concretely exemplifying the tactics of witness of the biblical people.

The timeliness of a study of both ROMANS 13 and REVELATION 13 is, I think, self-evident. Not only are the issues of conscience and obedience respecting the church and the nation in the forefront in America, albeit in mighty confusion, but much the same is the case in other societies. In Brazil, in Chile, in Korea, in China, in Taiwan, in the Philippines, in South Africa, in Kenya, in Tanzania, in Spain, in Italy, in Poland, in East Germany, in the Soviet Union—and, most poignantly, in Israel—these are immediate matters. That fact should caution American Christians not to be voguish and not to be chauvinistic, as so often they have been in the past, in attempting to cope with them.

Furthermore, one must keep in mind that the ruling authorities, as well as biblical people, are active in trying to determine these issues. I have mentioned earlier that I became persuaded to do this book while engaged in writing *An Ethic for Christians and Other Aliens in a Strange Land.*

That was no conclusion abstractly reached. It was mainly occasioned by the actual political situation in which *An Ethic* was written. On the very day that Daniel Berrigan, S.J., then a political fugitive because of his opposition to the war in Southeast Asia and his resistance to the war regime, was seized at the home of Anthony Towne and myself on Block Island by the federal police, I was typing the manuscript of that book. Subsequent to Berrigan's capture, Towne and I were subjected to harrassment, official defamation and surveillance by the authorities, including a remarkable incident in which a government agent, once again intruding upon my work on *An Ethic,* sought to interrogate me about theology and politics. He began the interview this way: "Dr. Stringfellow, you're a theologian." (I thought his introit faintly sarcastic.) "Doesn't the Bible say you must obey the Emperor?" His query startled me, I admit, not so much for its thrust as for the evidence it gave of how minutely the ruling powers scrutinize citizens. I could not concede the simplistic premise about the Bible which his question assumed, and I rebuked him about this, taking perhaps forty-five minutes to do so. During the discourse, he wilted visibly, and, when I paused momentarily, he abruptly excused himself and departed. This was some disappointment to me, for I had only just begun to respond to the multifarious implications of the issue he had raised. The episode contributed to my conviction to write this book.

William Stringfellow

The Epiphany, 1976
Block Island, Rhode Island

THE LETTER OF PAUL TO THE ROMANS

Chapter 12

I appeal to you therefore, brethren, by the mercies of God, to present your bodies as a living sacrifice, holy and acceptable to God, which is your spiritual worship. ²Do not be conformed to this world but be transformed by the renewal of your mind, that you may prove what is the will of God, what is good and acceptable and perfect.

³For by the grace given to me I bid every one among you not to think of himself more highly than he ought to think, but to think with sober judgment, each according to the measure of faith which God has assigned him.

⁴For as in one body we have many members, and all the members do not have the same function, ⁵so we, though many, are one body in Christ, and individually members one of another. ⁶Having gifts that differ according to the grace given to us, let us use them: if prophecy, in proportion to our faith; ⁷if service, in our serving; he who teaches, in his teaching; ⁸he who exhorts, in his exhortation; he who contributes, in liberality; he who gives aid, with zeal; he who does acts of mercy, with cheerfulness.

⁹Let love be genuine; hate what is evil, hold fast to what is good; ¹⁰love one another with brotherly affection; outdo one another in showing honor. ¹¹Never flag in zeal, be aglow with the Spirit, serve the Lord. ¹²Rejoice in your hope, be patient in tribulation, be constant in prayer. ¹³Contribute to the needs of the saints, practice hospitality.

¹⁴Bless those who persecute you; bless and do not curse them. ¹⁵Rejoice with those who rejoice, weep with those who weep. ¹⁶Live in harmony with one another; do not be haughty, but associate with the lowly; never be conceited.

[17]*Repay no one evil for evil, but take thought for what is noble in the sight of all.* [18]*If possible, so far as it depends upon you, live peaceably with all.* [19]*Beloved, never avenge yourselves, but leave it to the wrath of God; for it is written, "Vengeance is mine, I will repay, says the Lord."* [20]*No, "if your enemy is hungry, feed him; if he is thirsty, give him drink; for by so doing you will heap burning coals upon his head."* [21]*Do not be overcome by evil, but overcome evil with good.*

Chapter 13

Let every person be subject to the governing authorities. For there is no authority except from God, and those that exist have been instituted by God. [2]*Therefore he who resists the authorities resists what God has appointed, and those who resist will incur judgment.* [3]*For rulers are not a terror to good conduct, but to bad. Would you have no fear of him who is in authority? Then do what is good, and you will receive his approval,* [4]*for he is God's servant for your good. But if you do wrong, be afraid, for he does not bear the sword in vain; he is the servant of God to execute his wrath on the wrongdoer.* [5]*Therefore one must be subject, not only to avoid God's wrath but also for the sake of conscience.* [6]*For the same reason you also pay taxes, for the authorities are ministers of God, attending to this very thing.* [7]*Pay all of them their dues, taxes to whom taxes are due, revenue to whom revenue is due, respect to whom respect is due, honor to whom honor is due.*

[8]*Owe no one anything, except to love one another; for he who loves his neighbor has fulfilled the law.* [9]*The commandments, "You shall not commit adultery, You shall not kill, You shall not steal, You shall not covet," and any other commandment, are summed up in this sentence, "You shall love your neighbor as yourself."* [10]*Love does no wrong to a neighbor; therefore love is the fulfilling of the law.*

[11]Besides this you know what hour it is, how it is full time now for you to wake from sleep. For salvation is nearer to us now than when we first believed; [12]the night is far gone, the day is at hand. Let us then cast off the works of darkness and put on the armor of light; [13]let us conduct ourselves becomingly as in the day, not in reveling and drunkenness, not in debauchery and licentiousness, not in quarreling and jealousy. [14]But put on the Lord Jesus Christ, and make no provision for the flesh, to gratify its desires.

THE REVELATION TO JOHN

Chapter 13

And I saw a beast rising out of the sea, with ten horns and seven heads, with ten diadems upon its horns and a blasphemous name upon its heads. [2]And the beast that I saw was like a leopard, its feet were like a bear's, and its mouth was like a lion's mouth. And to it the dragon gave his power and his throne and great authority. [3]One of its heads seemed to have a mortal wound, but its mortal wound was healed, and the whole earth followed the beast with wonder. [4]Men worshiped the dragon, for he had given his authority to the beast, and they worshiped the beast, saying, "Who is like the beast, and who can fight against it?"

[5]And the beast was given a mouth uttering haughty and blasphemous words, and it was allowed to exercise authority for forty-two months; [6]it opened its mouth to utter blasphemies against God, blaspheming his name and his dwelling, that is, those who dwell in heaven. [7]Also it was allowed to make war on the saints and to conquer them. And au-

thority was given it over every tribe and people and tongue and nation, ⁸and all who dwell on earth will worship it, every one whose name has not been written before the foundation of the world in the book of life of the Lamb that was slain. ⁹If any one has an ear, let him hear:

> ¹⁰If any one is to be taken captive,
>   to captivity he goes;
> if any one slays with the sword,
>   with the sword must he be slain,

Here is a call for the endurance and faith of the saints.

¹¹Then I saw another beast which rose out of the earth; it had two horns like a lamb and it spoke like a dragon. ¹²It exercises all the authority of the first beast in its presence, and makes the earth and its inhabitants worship the first beast, whose mortal wound was healed. ¹³It works great signs, even making fire come down from heaven to earth in the sight of men; ¹⁴and by the signs which it is allowed to work in the presence of the beast, it deceives those who dwell on earth, bidding them make an image of the beast which was wounded by the sword and yet lived; ¹⁵and it was allowed to give breath to the image of the beast so that the image of the beast should even speak, and to cause those who would not worship the image of the beast to be slain. ¹⁶Also it causes all, both small and great, both rich and poor, both free and slave, to be marked on the right hand or the forehead, ¹⁷so that no one can buy or sell unless he has the mark, that is, the name of the beast or the number of its name. ¹⁸This calls for wisdom: let him who has understanding reckon the number of the beast, for it is a human number, its number is six hundred and sixty-six.

chapter one

Let every person be subject to the governing au-
thorities. For there is no authority except from
God, and those that exist have been instituted by
God. Therefore he who resists the authorities re-
sists what God has appointed, and those who resist
will incur judgment.

Romans 13:1–2

And I saw a beast rising out of the sea, with ten
horns and seven heads, with ten diadems upon its
horns and a blasphemous name upon its heads.
And the beast that I saw was like a leopard, its
feet were like a bear's, and its mouth was like a
lion's mouth. And to it the dragon gave his power
and his throne and great authority. One of its
heads seemed to have a mortal wound, but its
mortal wound was healed, and the whole earth
followed the beast with wonder. Men worshiped
the dragon, for he had given his authority to the
beast, and they worshiped the beast saying, "Who
is like the beast, and who can fight against it?"

Revelation 13:1–4

The Vocation of Political Authority

The elementary reason why issues of conscience and obedience in relation either to the nation or to the church are attended by consternation is a presumption, implicit or unstated, that there is a singular proposition in terms of which such questions can be resolved, despite disparate circumstances in which they arise.

Commonly it is supposed that there inheres, somewhere within the corpus of the gospel, a great fixed principle which—once truly apprehended and appropriately formulated—is capable of application and implementation whenever and wherever problems of conscience or claims of obedience in nation or in church require a stand by those aspiring to be faithful in the biblical task in history.

This notion, which is particularly, though by no means uniquely, ensconced in American Christendom, and, given that ethos, is curiously characteristic of pietists as well as activists, is blameworthy for frustration, confusion, mischief and tragedy frequently associated with that which purports to be the Christian witness in the world.

The presupposition is confounding because it is categorically false. It is a radical distortion of the gospel which, when pursued, dissipates the genius of the biblical life in this world. There is no such simplistic principle in biblical faith to be located, isolated, applied, and implemented in answer to any, much less every, question of conscience or obedience. The gospel is no superethic.

The imposition of this false presumption upon scraps of Scripture accounts for the frequent abuse of citations from Romans 13:1–7 or 1 Peter 3:17 or Luke 20:25, or other passages which name political authority at the behest of rulers or their courtesans.

Nor is the problem obviated by resorting to so-called proximate or provisional norms, as some suppose; it is only thereby evaded.

Instead of proposition or principle, the biblical witness offers precedent and parable. The Bible does not propound guidelines but relates events; the biblical ethic does not construct syllogisms but tells stories; the gospel is not confined in verities but confesses the viability of the Word of God. The biblical responses to issues of conscience and obedience are empirical and historic or else they are sacramental and portentous. In either style or instance, they exemplify and edify decisions and actions rather than predetermining or otherwise abstracting them.

The Vocation of the Word of God

If this distinction seems fastidious it is because it is basic and characteristic and not because it is either esoteric or pedantic. The concern it signifies is for the biblical credibility of the Incarnation, that is, of the primal status of the participation of the Word of God in common history. It is the event of the Incarnation, at once imminent truth and ultimate reality appertaining to the whole of creation as human beings perceive and encounter the same, which is definitive for the biblical witness in this world. It is the confession of the militance of the Word of God in this time and in this place as much as consummately which constitutes the mature ethical knowledge of biblical people. There is no norm, no ideal, no grandiose principle from which hypothetical, preconceived or pretentious answers can be derived because— to the biblical mind—there are no disincarnate issues; there are only actual questions requiring historic response on the part of persons and of principalities. There are only those decisions and actions which are judged, freely, in the presence of the Word of God in history.

To speak or act confessionally, coherently, biblically, in problems of conscience or obedience in nation or church— for that matter, to deal in biblical terms with ethics at all— is, thus, an endeavor at radical variance from the way in which such issues are posited in the world. Contrary to worldly conceptions of ethics, the biblical style forswears preemption of the office of God, does not feign coincidence with the mind of God, patiently abstains from claims of precognition of the judgment of the Word of God. Instead, of being vain, precocious or premature, the ethical activity of biblical people literally risks the judgment of the Word of God, or simply relies upon God's grace, or, as its most essential attribute, esteems the autonomy and freedom of God's will.

Some, I am aware, may cite, here, prophetic tradition especially as that is known in the Old Testament. What of those who confronted the professed people of God, crying *Thus saith the Lord!* ? I am neither unmindful nor ungrateful for the prophets, but I receive and affirm the New Testament as the perfection (that is to say, completion or fulfillment) of the Old Testament, so that I do not listen to the prophets of old in a vacuum, as if in ignorance of the New Testament. I do not find Amos or Jeremiah, or their peers, incongruous to Jesus Christ, or, further, to Paul or the author of Revelation and their peers. I hear prophetic utterance, then and also now, rebuking the impatience and idolatry of the people, exposing their religious vanity and moral legalism, and denouncing their recalcitrance to the viability of the Word of God. I notice the prophets admonishing the people that every creature—a nation no less than a human being—is subject here and now to God's sovereignty, reiterating that every thought and act or omission is under judgment, and calling for that repentance in which the new life of the holy nation is constituted. Biblically, the mark of authenticity, or prophetism is comprehension of the godliness of God and unbegrudged awe for the vocation of the Word of God in history. That reverence for the prerogatives of God is signified in the prophetic attribution which commonly follows the herald *Thus saith the Lord!* "I am the Lord thy God!"

In a comparable vein, the gift of the law is frequently mentioned as if to ignore the way in which the law is transfigured both in the ministry of Jesus and in his direct address to the subject in the Sermon on the Mount. (Matt. 5:17–48)

In the works of Jesus can be seen the very fulfillment of the law; while the Sermon shows how all persons stand under the judgment of the law of the Word of God as it is fulfilled in Jesus Christ. This is anticipated in the prophetic witness in its honor of the office of the Word of God in history. And, later, it is the authority for Paul's ministry as an Apostle and the passionate, reiterated theme of his teaching and nurture of the church and its members. (Cf. Rom. 10, 11; Gal. 3.)

It is the recognition of God's affirmation of himself in the midst of history in this world which becomes the introit for all issues of conscience and obedience, rather than any derivation and formulation, however solemn, of any ethical proposition or great principle. It is that acknowledgment which makes vocation the subject of ethics. It is that sensibility to the integrity of God as God which undoes the profound confusion concerning the vocation of humans and of nations and of all other creatures. Repeated, again, doctrinally (if perhaps more quaintly) the attempt to cope with questions of conscience and obedience in nation and in church begins in confession of the Incarnation.

At the outset, the focus is upon the vocation of the Word of God in this world. Yet, with that starting point, the realm of ethical activity implicates the vocation of all of life throughout creation simultaneously. Ethics has, essentially, to do with the exercise of vocation—with name and identification, selfhood and relationship, capability and function, place and purpose—for institutions and authorities as well as persons. This means, so far as human beings are concerned, that decisions and actions of conscience and obedience encompass and utilize the full diversity of gifts or talents indigenous to human life, while at the same time eschewing delusions of divinity which exceed and corrupt those very gifts, and resisting the comparable pretensions of godly status insinuated incessantly by the nations or other assorted principalities and powers.

That ethical deliberation originates vocationally and, for humans, engages every capacity pertinent to living humanly —neither more nor less—should, as it seems to me, in itself occasion suspicion of any ethical methodology which narrows, distorts, suppresses or denies any human capability or the diversity of gifts within human life. In other words, any ethical system which is settled and stereotyped, uniform and preclusive, neat and predictable is both dehumanizing and pagan—that is, literally, unbiblical. Such schemas misconstrue the significance of vocation in creation, inflating the role of the principalities while vitiating the human vocation; they issue in blasphemy, to use the word REVELATION cites so often, in cursing and usurping the vocation of the Word of God in the present age.

Creation, Fall, and the Significance of Vocation

The comprehension of vocation as elementary to ethics, to every problem of conscience or obedience whether in nation or in church, recalls explicitly the biblical stories of creation and of fallen creation. (Gen. 1–3; cf. Dietrich Bonhoeffer, *Creation and Fall*, NY: Macmillan, 1959).

I refer to these Genesis narratives as stories deliberately because the matter of their historicity is irrelevant to the truth which they convey. The perennial controversies associated with the question of the historical status of these texts are, it appears to me, a dissipation which, when in-

dulged, obscures what is most significant about the Genesis
stories of creation and fall, namely, the empirical credibility
of the description they furnish of life in this world.

Furthermore, those insistent upon literalistic interpretations of these passages succumb to a temptation to belittle
the Word of God in their very attempt to uphold the dignity
of the Word of God. To suppose that these stories happened
in time denies the transcendence of time characteristic of
the relationship of the Word of God to this world which the
Genesis texts bespeak.

Put another way, time, as humans perceive and suffer it,
is itself an aspect of fallen reality, a signal of the activity
of death, a most familiar and oppressive feature of the reign
of death in the world. In the participation of the Word of
God in history—in time—the Word of God is not somehow
diminished or can not be confined, but still retains freedom
from the parameters of time, transfigures time, abolishes
time, embodies eternity in time, redeems time. To refer to
the Word of God in temporal terms (which is the only language humans now have) is always, therefore, quaint and
stylistic, a manner of speaking, a metaphor, a parable. In
this way, human beings can be spared the temptations to
possess or control, restrict or define the Word of God, the
mystery inherent in truth remains viable and inexhaustible,
and the efficacy of the redemptive power of the presence of
the Word of God in this world is respected.

So it is that I urge those who would unintentionally
demean or inadvertently deaden the Word of God by impos-
ing a literalistic rubric upon Scripture to be even *more*
earnest than they now profess to be toward the Bible and,
thence, to behold these stories of creation and fall in Genesis
as descriptions, the truth of which is not contingent upon
their mundane historicity but which, far more cogent than
that, is universally and repetitiously attested empirically
in common history.

The truth of the Genesis creation story is not that God
made human beings on the first Saturday but that the life
of the whole of creation originates in the utterance of the

Word of God. Life, in the inception, is a gift. In the event of creation, each and every creature and each and every aspect of the totality of creation receives life in integrity and relationship, in harmony and fulfillment within the scope of God's sovereignty. Persons and principalities, all the creatures, all realities or elements of creation are named by the Word of God. Each is beneficiary of an identity, capacity, purpose, and place in conjunction with that of everyone and everything else. In other words, in creation *vocation* issues from the Word of God. Still more precisely, in the biblical description of creation, the vocation of God becomes definitive of the vocation of human life and of that of institutions and nations and other creatures and of all things whatever.

Despite the variegations of life in creation, surpassing the particularity and detail peculiar to the varieties of creaturehood or the diversities of created status, there is, in the biblical insight, a singular feature shared throughout creation. That hallmark of the vocation of the whole of creation is the glorification of the Word of God as the source of life: the adoration of the Creator, the praise and gratitude of creation for the generosity of God, the celebration of life as a gift, or, simply, the worship of God. The worship of God is the elemental and consummate connotation of vocation for the whole of creation and for the various specific forms of life within creation.

In the biblical story, the equation of vocation and worship is expressed in the preeminence attributed to human life. The Word of God bestows upon humans dominion over the rest of creation. Dominion, here, is not to be mistaken for domination; the rule or governance to which human life is appointed, in the creation story, is one in which the distinctive human faculties are engaged and fulfilled in signifying the active sovereignty of the Word of God to the whole of creation so that every other aspect of the life of creation is related and realized. It is not for the aggrandizement of human life that dominion is conferred, but for the sake of the perfect life of all of creation, which is exemplified as worship. The service to human beings, the enhancement of human life in society rendered by the rest of creation under human dominion is appropriated in worship—in the free, conscientious, and glad confession of humans that the life of the whole of creation is the gift of the Word of God.

All of this is spoiled and distorted in fallen creation. The biblical story of the fall bespeaks the renunciation of life as a gift; the rejection of the event of the Word of God calling life into being and naming the creatures, and everything else, and vesting dominion in human life; the abandonment of worship and its displacement with blasphemy and idolatry, and the radical moral confusion as to vocation affecting everyone and all things in creation. It is the repudiation of life as the gratuity of the Word of God which describes sin in its essential attribute; the consequence of sin is consignment to death. In sin human dominion is lost; the vocation of human life is profoundly disoriented; the rest of creation (including, notably, the principalities and powers) suffers similar chaos. The vocation of creation is usurped. In the fall, the reign of death is pervasive and militant, it spares no life whatever: every relationship is broken or corrupted or diminished to violence, antiworship is endemic for institutions and nations as much as persons, time means confinement to the power of death, instead of possessing dominion over creation human life is enslaved to and dominated by the rest of creation. In fallen creation, the power of death appears triumphant over the existence of this world.

The fallenness of the nations and powers is conjunctive with the fallenness of humanity, but it is not dependent or derivative. The principalities are autonomous in relation to humans, they are created beings or realities in their own right, not simply projections of collective human life, and their demonic character as fallen powers is no mere consequence of human sin either personal or corporate. (See *An Ethic* . . . page 75ff.)

So the Bible treats them, and so, I observe, they are as common experience confronts them. It is misleading, hence, to speak of an institution or nation or political regime becoming demonic, as if its fallen character were, somehow, contingent upon human action or omission which precipitates the corruption or decadence of a principality. Furthermore, such a view, which has had great vogue in moral theology in American Christendom, not only denies the creaturely status of the principalities and powers, but also denies that the whole creation originates in the Word of God. It denigrates God as Creator by exaggerating the potency and scope of human sin.

The Lordship of Christ in Fallen Creation

The biblical witness, as the Gospel according to St. John reminds, does not end in the saga of the fall. The biblical testament is completed in Jesus Christ. Jesus Christ means that though the fall ruins creation, the fall does not dissipate the grace of God. Jesus Christ means that though human beings and, indeed, the whole of creation reject life as the gift of the Word of God, the Word of God is not thereby retracted or refuted or revoked. Christ means that although in fallen creation vocation is distorted and worship is scandalized, the sovereignty of God is neither disrupted nor aborted. Christ means that in the fall, in the midst of the reign of death in time, within the common history of this world, the Word of God nevertheless acts to restore life to the whole of creation. Jesus Christ means that the freedom of God is not curtailed by the fall and not intimidated by the thrall of death, but elects to redeem creation from the power of death. Jesus Christ means the embodiment in human life, now, in this world, of the abundance of the Word of God for salvation from sin and redemption from death for all creation.

Thus it has come to pass that biblical people esteem Jesus Christ as Lord. This is not, as is sometimes erroneously supposed, a title designating the divinity of Christ; it, rather, explicitly explains the humanity of Jesus as the one who epitomizes the restoration of dominion over the rest of creation vested in human life by the sovereignty of the Word of God during the epoch of the fall. Jesus Christ as Lord signifies the renewed vocation of human life in reconciliation with the rest of creation.

Hence, those who live in Christ and who honor Christ as

Lord, who are members of the body of the Church of Christ, live in the present age as a "new creation" (2 Cor. 5:17).

It will be, I hope, clear that to reach an affirmation as to the essential character of the church in this way has no basic similarity to the ways of human idealism, the practice of religion, or the entertainment of speculations and visions. The claim of the church that it represents in history restored creation is not contingent at all upon virtue in the church but upon the freedom of the Word of God in this world. It is that, I believe, which is the rudimentary and constant cause of tension and friction—the New Testament sometimes refers to *warfare*—between the church and the world, particularly between the church and the nation or the state or other ruling principalities and powers.

At the crux of that incessant conflict is the vocational issue, and, concretely, the discernment which the church, as the exemplar of renewed creation, practices concerning the vocation of political authority. In that witness, the church confesses, on behalf of every nation or state or regime that political authority has a vocation, as every creature does. The church, as it were, remembers that vocation and honors it duly by confessing that political authority is "ordained" or "appointed" by God. Yet, simultaneously, in the midst of the anarchy which is the fall, in this perishing age, while political authority remains beholden to the power of death, that confession of the vocation of political authority *always* upholds the preeminence of dominion restored to human life or, in other words, *always* affirms the Lordship of Jesus Christ. But if the church is faithful to Jesus Christ as Lord, can the church ever support political authority in status quo?

chapter two

For rulers are not a terror to good conduct, but to bad. Would you have no fear of him who is in authority? Then do what is good, and you will receive his approval, for he is God's servant for your good.

Romans 13:3–4a

Then I saw another beast which rose out of the earth; it had two horns like a lamb and it spoke like a dragon. It exercises all the authority of the first beast in its presence, and makes the earth and its inhabitants worship the first beast, whose mortal wound was healed. It works great signs, even making fire come down from heaven to earth in the sight of men; and by the signs which it is allowed to work in the presence of the beast, it deceives those who dwell on earth, bidding them make an image for the beast which was wounded by the sword and yet lived.

Revelation 13:11–14

chapter two

The
Problem
of Political
Legitimacy

Viewing the passages concerning political authority in
ROMANS and in REVELATION in the context of the biblical stories of creation and fall and the biblical witness to
God's redemptive initiative in fallen creation does not dis-
solve all tension or contrast between these texts. It does
concentrate on the issue of the vocation of political authority in each of them. It does emphasize the coherence of the
two passages. The references in ROMANS to political authority
as instituted by God and as God's servant recall that political authority—along with every other creature—has authenticity and fulfillment of its own integrity and capacity in
life in worship, which is to say, in recognition and adoration
of the sovereignty of the Word of God within the purview of
human dominion. On the other hand, the profound distortion
(though not obliteration) of that very vocation for the
fallen political principalities is described, in REVELATION, in
the grotesque imagery of predatory beasts, crowned with
blasphemous names, cursing the Word of God and assault-
ing those who do profess and trust the sovereignty of the
Word of God in this world.

The repudiation of the gift of life and the consignment to the power of death which is the reality of the fall, as has been mentioned, does not avert or abort or estop redemption. The Word of God persists in fallen creation—inherent or residual, hidden or secreted, latent or discreet, mysterious and essential. (cf. Rom. 1:20; James 1:21.) Having the eyes to behold that presence of the Word, or having the ears to listen to the Word, having the gift of discernment, is, indeed, the most significant way in which Christians are distinguished from other human beings in this world. Yet there is also a sense in which the Word of God, perseverant despite the fall, is attested in the futility of blasphemy: in the impotence of political authority against the power of death, in the incapacity of political authority—no matter how beneficent or how beguiling—to achieve the renewal of creation or to approximate the kingdom of God, or, for that matter, to even implement its own mundane ideals and ideologies. It is this confounding of the antiworship indulged by political authority, and by all fallen principalities and powers, which paradoxically confirms the biblical insight that the sovereignty of the Word of God becomes historically notorious in the resurrection of Christ and which inadvertently substantiates the biblical faith that Christ's dominion is triumphant in judgment of political authority and of all creatures and all things whatsoever (Rom. 12:19).

So it is, as Karl Barth reminded us, that Pilate, despite himself and his political office, and, by the Gospel accounts, virtually beside himself, when confronted by Christ names Christ as Lord (Karl Barth, *Church and State,* London: SCM Press, 1939).

Though he is overcome by apprehension and is filled with begrudgement, Pilate certifies the accusation and, lo, *it is the truth!* The very words by which political authority condemns Christ confess Christ's authority. The trial before Pilate is not a disconnected incident; in the same vein are the encounters between Herod and Christ, or the dialectics concerning Caesar and Christ, or the episodes in which the demoniacs suffer exorcism, or the beleagurement of Christ in the wilderness by death incarnate as the devil.

That these, or any feigned rulers of the present age recognize, if sardonically, the Lordship of Christ is not a matter of predestinarianism. It is a wondrous sign of how resolute the Word of God in history is, of how transient and empty— for all its haughty sound and style—blasphemy is, and also of how the witness of the biblical society which lives in this world in Christ is recognized by political authority as ridicule and rebuke and awesome admonishment.

What I write, here, I realize, departs from that which has come to be taught as traditional exegesis of ROMANS, where ROMANS has been treated in a void and, specifically, where ROMANS 13:1-7 has been examined separately and, meanwhile, REVELATION 13 has been ignored or suppressed or deemed esoteric. That only points to how both passages, in traditional usage, have been too much historically conditioned: ROMANS has been interpreted in conformance with supposed necessities to sanction incumbent political regimes, whether of the fourth century or of the twentieth; REVELATION has been dismissed as pertinent just to a certain first century regime or else has been construed as apocalyptic fantasy without historic reference to any regime. Still, if my comprehension of ROMANS in relation to REVELATION varies from more prevalent or customary interpretations of either passage, I do not conceive that to be a matter of blunt opposition but of distinctions which I count significant as between my own understanding and the traditional view.

The Ambiguity of Legitimacy

Prominent among such distinctions is the way in which the vocational issue for political authority is narrowed— sometimes to the degree that it amounts to omission—to the problem of political legitimacy. By that rubric, the obedience of Christians to political authority is conditioned upon its so-called legitimacy. But when is political authority legitimate? When does a nation have a status which may be affirmed as instituted or ordained of God? Or when does a state have a function which can be considered as servanthood to God? And when are those who rule—emperors or presidents—parliaments or police—due honor not alone because of fear, because they wield the sword, because they command means to intimidate, dominate and coerce human beings, but as a matter of conscience? ←

Within the American ethos, it should be noted, these have never been abstract questions either for those who profess the gospel or for those who do not. The founding premises of the nation define legitimacy in government both with respect to a rule deemed so obnoxious to human life in society that it was to be resisted and overthrown, in the Declaration of Independence, and, thereafter, in the limitations upon political authority and the institutionalization of public accountability published in the Constitution. According to the Declaration and the Constitution, political legitimacy relates to both how political power is used and to how it is established, incumbency in itself not being sufficient to validate the exercise of political authority.

The matter permeates the American experience as a nation and society, with its peculiar admixture of theology and politics, and it lately has emerged again in the crises attending Watergate and the war in Southeast Asia. Hence, when the Bill of Impeachment was uttered against Richard Nixon, the *New York Times* stated that the nation could "look forward with confidence to the further working out of its constitutional processes for the *restoration of legitimacy* in the highest executive office". (The *New York Times*, August 4, 1974, Sec. E, p. 16, italics added). If legitimacy of political authority was, thus, at stake, it must necessarily be asked whether the aborting of the Nixon impeachment by the pardon dispensed by Gerald Ford after Ford had been appointed to succession by Nixon leaves the nation deprived of "the restoration of legitimacy in the highest executive office". Or, again, the opposition (notably that of confessing Christians) to the war and to the war enterprise in Southeast Asia during the late nineteen sixties upheld the position that the criminal policy and unconstitutional conduct of the war exposed incumbent political authority (first the Johnson administration and then that of Nixon) as illegitimate. It is this assessment which occasioned the witness of the Berrigan brothers becoming fugitives at the time they had been ordered to submit to imprisonment. For them to have voluntarily surrendered to illegitimate authority would have condoned it. For the Berrigans, as well as other Christians, there could be no obedience to illegitimate power. It is, I think, edifying to remember this now because, among other things, it means that many of those who resisted did so not as cowards or weirdos, far out radicals or malcontents, traitors or rebels, but, in fact, resisted to uphold a quite traditional view of political legitimacy. The very citizens the war regime was most anxious to watch and spy upon, defame and persecute, humiliate and ostracize, prosecute and punish were those who acted to restore legitimacy in government so that political authority could be conscientiously honored in the nation.

The construction of obedience to political authority in terms of legitimacy is familiar enough in the American context in the origins of the nation and up to the present time, and there is some support for it in the biblical texts at hand. The ROMANS passage furnishes a basis in its reference to political authority as a "terror" to "bad" conduct, a statement which would be nonsensical if it did not apply to the conduct of political authority as such. If ROMANS may be said to designate legitimate political authority, REVELATION may be said to describe illegitimate political authority.

Commentators who must be respected as venerable and influential have concentrated upon how legitimacy can be determined so as to set forth the parameters of political obedience for Christians. Grotius, whose view coincides with the simple association of ROMANS with legitimacy and REVELATION with illegitimacy, writes: "The Apostle throughout refers only to power justly exercised. He does not enter into the subject of tyranny and oppression."

The classical statement concerning obedience as contingent upon the legitimacy of political authority comes from John Calvin's *Commentary on Romans*. This was a work completed, it may be significant to notice, before Calvin himself became a magistrate in Geneva. Of ROMANS 13:1–7, he said:

> Understand further, that powers are from God . . .
> because he has appointed them for the legitimate
> and just government of the world. For though
> tyrannies and unjust exercise of power, as they
> are full of disorder, are not an ordained govern-
> ment; yet the right of government is ordained by
> God for the wellbeing of mankind. As it is lawful
> to repel wars and to seek remedies for other evils,
> hence the Apostle commands us willingly and
> cheerfully to respect and honour the right and
> authority of magistrates, as useful to men . . .

To require obedience to political authority where there is
legitimacy, and to relate legitimacy to just government
seems straightforward enough, until it is realized that the
ambiguity associated with determining legitimacy has been
transmitted to the word "just". The quandry about the
indefinite meaning of legitimacy is hardly resolved by the
relativity of what may be deemed just. In practice, of course,
the more specific connotations of just political rule are
furnished situationally or existentially, in spite of the ra-
tionalist pretenses that pure or abstract and immutable
definitions of political justice can be divined.

At that, there is some redundancy in the meaning of just
government insofar as similar circumstances recur from
time to time. For example, a minister in New England
sought to be concrete about this matter in a sermon; his
remarks were informed by the immediate political situation in America, which was that of 1770, when the revolutionary cause against the British crown was fermenting.
With little amendment, his homily would have been
appropos in 1974, when the Watergate scandal unfolded:

> [Rulers] are obliged to seek the welfare of the
> people and exert all their powers to promote the
> common interest. This continual solicitude for the
> common good, however depressing it may appear,
> is what rulers of every degree have taken upon
> themselves, and in justice to the people, in faith-
> fulness to God, they must either sustain it with
> fidelity or resign their office. . . .

Fidelity to the public requires that the laws be
as plain and explicit as possible, that the less
knowing may understand and not be ensnared by √
them, while the artful evade their force. Mysteries ·
of law and government may be a cloak of unright-
eousness. . . .

The just ruler will not fear to have his public conduct critically inspected, but will choose to recommend himself to the approbation of every man.
√ As he expects to be obeyed for conscience sake,
√ he will require nothing inconsistent with its dic-
tates . . . (Sermon of the Rev. Samuel Cooke,
Cambridge, Mass., May 30, 1770.)

Somewhat earlier, in 1750, another American clergyman,
Jonathan Mayhew, felt impelled, because of the political
situation in the colonies, to exegete ROMANS 13. (He rendered his own translation, which some may conclude con-
venienced his exegesis.) If, today, his views sound familiar
it is because he bespeaks a liberation theology similar to
that now articulate throughout the Third World:

[I]t has often been asserted that the Scriptures in
general, and the passage under consideration in
particular, makes all resistance to princes a crime,
in any case whatever. If they turn tyrants . . .
we must not pretend to right ourselves, unless it
be by prayers, and tears and humble entreaties. . . .

[T]he duty of unlimited obedience, whether active or passive, can be argued neither from the
manner of expression here used, nor from the
general scope and design of the passage. . . .

If rulers are a terror to good works and not to
the evil; if they are not ministers for good to
society but for evil and distress by violence and
oppression; if they execute wrath upon sober,
peaceable persons who do their duty as members
of society, and suffer rich . . . knaves to escape
with impunity; if, instead of attending continually
upon the good work of advancing the public

> welfare—if this be the case, it is plain that the
> apostle's argument for submission does not reach
> them. . . . If those who bear the title of civil rulers
> do not perform the duty of civil rulers but act
> directly counter to the sole end and design of
> their office; if they injure and oppress their sub-
> jects instead of defending their rights and doing
> them good, they have not the least pretense to
> be honored, obeyed and rewarded, according to
> the apostle's argument. . . .

Even if one must look to actual events to dispel vague-
ness and supply specificity to legitimate and/or just political
authority, that does not entirely meet the ambiguities of
these terms. There still lingers, for one matter, the necessity
of distinguishing legitimacy from lawfulness. These are not
synonyms, though they are often confused, and such confusion becomes critical when it becomes a factor in attempting to understand ROMANS 13 or REVELATION 13. Consider,
as an example, the regime of George III. It seems to have
been, at first glance, a lawful government in the sense that
its incumbency was achieved by lawful process, by the
prescribed tradition or constitution for succession to the
British throne, rather than by revolution or coup d' etat. Yet
lawful accession to office and power does not in itself ensure
that the government remains lawful. In fact, though probably no one in Britain and few, if any, in America would
have challenged the lawfulness of the enthronement of
George III, some in America and others in Britain did come
to question whether the rule of George III with respect to
the colonies violated the *British* constitution and thereby
became unlawful or was to that extent unlawful, regardless
of the lawfulness of the succession. That, indeed, was one
of the issues raised in the First Continental Congress and it
was introduced not by advocates of American independence
but by those who sought a way to remain loyal to the crown.
For that matter, it was debated in Parliament.

Meanwhile, the revolutionary cause, as Jonathan Mayhew
had foreshadowed by a quarter of a century, was rationalized by imputing illegitimacy—as distinct from unlawful-

ness—to the rule of George III. That had more to do with
theology than law because it was asserted that political
authority is or ought to be limited by rights self-evident
and basic to human beings sanctioned by God over and
above any boundaries of political authority provided by the
law of a society. As vigorously as this doctrine was promul-
gated, in the Declaration of Independence, in the articles
of some of the colonial assemblies, and in a profusion of
tracts, it was by no measure accepted as obvious or self-
validating and many Americans continued to submit to the
rule of George III as legitimate, as well as lawful, just as,
of course, most of the British people did.

What do we have here? We find one historic regime which
can be and which was, in fact, simultaneously deemed legitimate and lawful, and illegitimate but lawful, and legitimate
but unlawful, and illegitimate and unlawful, according to
which faction in which country to which the regime pertains
beholds it. Similar alternatives could be mentioned if one
examined the emergent government in revolutionary America. On one hand, the rebellion would be unlawful, yet, as
the American polemists argued, it was legitimate; presum-
ably George III found it both unlawful and illegitimate;
some American Tories thought the colonists' grievances lawful, but the revolutionary war illegitimate; if, however, the
revolution be assessed as legitimate, wherein did it also
become lawful—When the war was won? When other nations accorded recognition? When the Constitution was
ratified? After the war of 1812?

Manifestly, legitimacy has little substantive definition
apart from that attributed to it historically, according to
the circumstances of a specific regime or particular ruler,
and empirically, relative to those governed and whether
they benefit or suffer under that political authority. This
has been notably the case in America when the issue of
legitimacy has been conceived as turning upon the incident
of suffrage. The notion is that the legitimacy of political
authority is verified by the existence of representative government elected by the people. Consent of the governed, to
use a traditional phrase, legitimatizes political authority.

This is an extension of Mayhew's position, save that recourse to revolution is deemed obviated by the capability for political change vested in the franchise.

It is an appealing idea, though questions linger as to whether a regime must then be counted illegitimate if suffrage is either precluded in practice or ineffectual as a means of political change. By this test, for instance, was the American government illegitimate through all the time that women were denied the right to vote? Or was it somewhat legitimate, but illegitimate so far as women were concerned? Similar queries must be asked respecting the rural and the urban poor, blacks, Indians, Chicanos, illiterates, certain immigrants—any who have ever been barred from enfranchisement by law or in fact. And, if the effectuality of voting is considered, a whole range of other questions must be confronted which dilute the straightforward sound of this test of legitimacy. The principal issue of that sort in America now is whether there remains a significant relationship between the right to vote and governing powers. The answer to that is, at the least, very dubious if one realistically observes the ruling initiative of extra-constitutional institutions like the Pentagon or the internal police or the Central Intelligence Agency which usually operate outside the rule of law, often in defiance of the elected government and its policies, and, seemingly, beyond accountability to citizens.

More than that, the emergence now of multinational and transnational conglomerates controlling the most basic resources requisite to life, and their operation beyond the regulatory capacities of nation–states, may de facto represent the new nations of the world, the ruling authorities of the world's *realpolitik*, superseding the old nations, like the United States, reigning utterly in terms of their own aggrandizement. If that be the analytical truth about the political domination of the world by these remarkable principalities, suffrage becomes meaningless because it is unconnected categorically with government.

The Meaning of Political Authority

This is enough to indicate why I find the interpretation

of obedience to political authority as turning upon the assessment of legitimacy—for all that it is represented as an objective test—extremely relative, heavily ambiguous, an artificial and unnecessary imposition upon the biblical texts, and unedifying where the concern and intent is witness to Christ as Lord.

Nor do the variables affecting legitimacy and illegitimacy, the lawful and the lawless in government exhaust the difficulties of this traditional usage with respect—topically—to either ROMANS 13 or REVELATION 13.

The ambiguity of political authority itself, and the terms commonly associated with it, cannot be ignored. One dimension of this further problem is exposed if the question is put—*what is the reality of political authority?* Does political authority necessarily imply reference to an actual regime or administration, as to the reign of the Emperor Caligula or to the rule of George III or to the presidency of Richard Nixon? Or may its import be to the "system"—to the institutional apparatus of government organized pursuant to a constitution or other charter or to the state in a functional sense? Or, again, is the reference to what may be designated "the nation"—the constellation of ethnic, geographic, cultural, ideational elements in which the tradition and ethos of a people in society is wrought and thence transmitted? Beyond that, is there a "spirit" of a nation which impinges upon political authority in each or any of the connotations mentioned? Or, for that matter, when political authority is named are the spirit of a nation, *and* a nation's ethos, *and* its basic institutionalization, *and*, also, this or that historic regime all implied or implicated to an extent that it is impracticable or arbitrary to attempt to sort them out and distinguish one from the others?

I am inclined toward this last construction in which multiple denotations are simultaneously indicated, though, in a given connection one or another may have greater prominence. I do not suppose one can speak, for example, of a specific president and his administration without some consciousness of the institution of the presidency in the Ameri-

can governmental system, and of the Constitution, and of
the nation's inheritance socially and ideologically and, indeed, of such a reality as the spirit of the American nation.
Nor do I think it possible to name the spirit of the nation as
abstruse cosmology without soon having to mention how
that spirit is conveyed and represented concretely in the nation's tradition and style, in charter and law, in political
institutions, in specific regimes, and, sometimes, in personifi-
cation in political incumbents.

Yet if this be so in common thought and talk when political authority is the subject, it occasions much ambiguity and
potential confusion for the comprehension of biblical passages, like those in ROMANS and in REVELATION which deal
with political authority. Sometimes the context or syntax
of a passage will furnish enlightenment as the sense in which
terms denoting political authority are used. But at times
diligent attention is not enough to clarify.

By way of illustration, the famous text in 1 Peter 2:17 has
been rendered in popular translation: *Honor all men. Love
the brotherhood. Fear God. Honor the emperor.* That translation has been repeatedly invoked (particularly by emperors) to elicit uncritical acquiescence or unquestioning
obedience to the emperor, that is, to a particular incumbent
ruler or regime. Hitler, and the ecclesiastics who supported
the Nazi administration in the 1930s relied heavily upon
this citation; I have related earlier in this book how the FBI
sought to intimidate me by resorting to the same text. Yet
conscientious scholarship lately yields a translation with
startlingly different implications than assorted emperors, or
pro-Nazi bishops, or the FBI impute to First Peter. In that
transliteration, the phrase *honor the emperor* reads *honor to
the sovereign!* (1 Pet. 2:17b NEB.) If that which is due
honor is the sovereign, as distinguished from either the
person of an incumbent or a particular regime, one might
readily find that in order to "honor the emperor" it becomes
necessary to oppose the emperor. That was, in fact, as I
have already noted, the burden of the Christian witness
against the war administration in America: the opposition
to the regime was a way of honoring the sovereign; to

expose the criminality and illegality of the war was an effort to uphold the Constitution, the rule of law, and accountability to people.

Inasmuch as ambiguity attends the identification of political authority so that the term carries many meanings and allusions which may, or may not, be able to be elucidated in context historically or linguistically or otherwise, that should <u>caution</u> both politicians and preachers against simplistic <u>readings</u> of the biblical passages pertinent to questions of conscience and obedience in the political realm.

The propriety of such caution is underscored in an edifying monograph which Clinton D. Morrison published in 1960 on ROMANS 13:1–7 under the title *The Powers That Be*. The paper deals with the relation of "earthly rulers" and "demonic powers" and it establishes that the textual references to political authority in ROMANS 13:1–7 imply not one or the other of these, but *both* in association. Morrison shows that this multiple or ambiguous meaning for political authority in ROMANS is verified, in part, in the time the text was composed in both Jewish cosmology as well as in the pagan or nonbiblical cosmologies then prevalent. As a matter of popular understanding, allusion in ROMANS to political authority would not solely indicate rulers or regimes but also be taken to refer to the demons or elemental spirits of the universe or angelic powers associated with the nations and, in turn, with governments and rulers. Morrison emphasizes the belief in a realm in creation of political beings was not distinctive to Christians, at the time of ROMANS, but, in one version or another, was generally shared. That magnifies, it seems to me, its significance for understanding ROMANS 13:1–7. In any case, I believe, biblical people must retain today essentially the same comprehension—even though others, as if more sophisticated, may think it peculiar.

This has already been affirmed in speaking of the vocation of political authority and of the disorientation of that vocation in fallen creation. At that, a related exposition, theologically and analytically, is found in *An Ethic for*

Christians and Other Aliens in a Strange Land based upon
the Babylon parable in the Book of Revelation (page 97ff.).

It is sufficient now to say, however, that the cosmological
insight attributable to Paul when he wrote the Letter to
the Romans, which was, as well, one which his readers held
and one more or less publicly accepted (*including incumbent rulers!*), precludes interpretations of the first seven
verses of ROMANS 13 as if they only had pertinence to obedience to whatever regime happens to occupy office, much
less an obligation of simplistic or automatic obedience to
the person of the ruler.

The Constantinian Status Quo

Paradoxically, subsequent to the writing of the Letter to
the Romans, Christians have, on one hand, forgotten or for-
saken a worldview or, more precisely, doctrines of creation
and of fallen creation, similar to Paul's, in which political
authority encompasses and conjoins the angelic powers and
the incumbent rulers. On the other hand, they have adopted
arbitrary or contrived criteria, such as that of legitimacy or
"just rule" in order to accommodate ROMANS 13:1-7 and
still allow occasional pretext for disobedience to political
authority. The result is deeply unsatisfactory and has often
failed to sustain a conscientious witness in relation to political authority. That indicates that there is need to renew a
biblical apprehension of political authority, in its manifold
allusions, to focus, as I have suggested, upon vocation as the
clue to conscience and obedience in nation and in church.
In doing so, particularly with regard to the institutionalization of Christianity in the West, and, in turn, the existence
of Christendom in America, it is necessary to account the
momentous impact of the Constantinian Arrangement.

By that accommodation, signaled by the conversion of the
emperor and the establishment of Christianity as the official
"religion" of the Roman empire, a comity between church
and nation was sponsored which, in various elaborations, still
prevails in the twentieth century. The incidents which occasioned the Constantinian Arrangement, as such, are not
as significant for contemporary Christians, or for either

church or state today, as the ethos spawned and nourished
by that comity and the mentality which has been engen-
dered and indoctrinated by it over so long a time. It is, put
plainly, an ethos which vests the existence of the church in
the preservation of the political status quo. This inbreeds
a mentality, affecting virtually all professed Christians, and
most citizens whether Christians or not, which regards it
as normative for the church's life to be so vested. And that
has caused radical confusions in the relations of church and
nation, church and state, church and regime. It has encour-
aged and countenanced stupid allegiance to political authority as if that were service to the church and, *a fortiori*, to
God. Venerable though it be, this accommodation, and the
way of conceiving of the juxtaposition of church and political authority which it has inculcated for so very long,
accounts more than anything else for the profound secularization of the church in the West and for the inception
of Christendom as the worldly embellishment of Christianity.

To put the same matter the other way around, it is the
Constantinian Arrangement which has fostered, in numerous versions and derivations, through the centuries, such a
religioning of the gospel that its biblical integrity is corrupted and such an acculturation of the church that it
becomes practically indistinguishable from the worldly
principalities so that both gospel and church become ad-
juncts or conveyances of civil religion, and of a mock-
sanctified status of political authority. In consequence,
contemporary Christians inherit the heaviest possible presumption of legitimacy favoring incumbent political rulers
and regimes and with that a supposed preemptive duty of
obedience to them which has been challenged only spasmodically.

I do not judge—I have neither vocation nor capability for
that—the complication of factors which weighed on the side
of the church concluding this comity with the empire. One
may speculate about various influences: the arrangement
ostensibly brought an end to the long era of the church's
persecution, for one consideration. Moreover, the mission to
evangelize the world might readily have been supposed

implemented by the conversion of the emperor. At that, there is some evidence in St. Paul's career as an evangelist— as early as when he wrote ROMANS—that he aspired himself to confront and convert the emperor though his apologetic was heard only by lesser officials like Felix, Festus, and Agrippa, and he is said to have converted only certain of Caesar's soldiers, his jailors, not Caesar himself.

The query occurs, indeed, whether Paul had so strenuous an aspiration to convert the emperor that this determined the substance of ROMANS 13:1–7.

There were other influences, too, including the effort, particularly in the first century, of the church to distinguish itself from the Jewish sects and notably from the zealotic parties of Judaism in the eyes of the ruling authorities.

These are all solemn considerations, and I do not ridicule them insofar as they may have been inducements arising in the early and apostolic eras of the church sanctioning eventually the Constantinian Arrangement. Anyway, history cannot be undone, this comity, whether misfortune, or worse, or not, is part of the inheritance of contemporary Christians—an immensely important happening which cannot be erased. That is why I treat it, here, as a political and theological issue, and why I suggest that, though history cannot be retracted, the inherited political and theological stance for the church, signified in the Constantinian accommodation, must be transcended: contemporary Christian people can be emancipated from the indoctrination of the Constantinian mentality and a biblical integrity can be renewed in the church. Amen

I construe the Constantinian comity as the historic reversal of the precedent established in the apostolic church regarding relations with political authority. In the first century, the Imperial authorities permitted a comity with various religious sects (including those of the Jews except for the zealots who advocated rebellion against the Roman rule) which safeguarded the practice of religion and religious premises and prerogatives of religious leaders so long as these were politically innocuous and did not disrupt or resist political authority. The church in the apostolic period could have conformed and become a beneficiary of this sort of comity, and controversy preoccupied the church, and the apostles of the church, about this. One formulation of the dispute concerned whether the church was, indeed, a sect of Judaism or whether it was distinguished in a way which required the church's faith and message to be dispersed throughout the world. Much of the deliberation of this issue revolved, of course, around St. Paul and the question of his authority as an apostle and his arguments for preaching the gospel to the gentiles. It is the persuasion of Paul, and the acceptance of his apostolic authority, together with the vision which St. Peter suffers concerning the ecumenical scope of the mission of the church in this world, which establish that the church is no mere sect, among many sects, and that the church cannot afford the accommodation with political authority which the sectarian comity conveyed. Rome perceives the calling of the church to the ecumenical mission accurately to be a threat to its political hegemony and, thereafter, the intimidation, defamation and harassment of the church escalates into persecution.

In this light, the promulgation of the Constantinian Arrangement represents a reversal, both politically and theologically, of the apostolic precedent of the juxtaposition of the church and political authority. The issue ever since, through both the glory and the tragedy of the church's presence in the world, has been whether the church can be free of the Constantinian comity and whether the apostolic precedent can be revived, and that, not so much for the sake of the church as for the sake of the world.

chapter three

But if you do wrong, be afraid, for he does not bear the sword in vain; he is the servant of God to execute his wrath on the wrongdoer. Therefore one must be subject, not only to avoid God's wrath but also for the sake of conscience.

Romans 13:4b–5

And the beast was given a mouth uttering haughty and blasphemous words, and it was allowed to exercise authority for forty-two months; it opened its mouth to utter blasphemies against God, blaspheming his name and his dwelling, that is, those who dwell in heaven.

Revelation 13:5–6

Anarchy, Apocalyptic Reality, and the Antichrist

There is another rationale for obedience to the powers that be which has the weight of traditional usage and has acquired much prestige throughout Christendom because it so conveniences the comity of church and political authority generally prevalent since the Constantinian Arrangement. Like the criteria of legitimacy, it has various versions, and, indeed, some have conceived of it as not just complementary or parallel to political legitimacy, but as a translation of legitimacy, or as a way of giving specific definition to legitimacy without entering into assessments about the policy or conduct of a regime or system.

This is the position and argument that obedience to political authority, practically identified as an incumbent administration, is requisite for Christians for the sake of the order which political authority imposes, supervises, and maintains. Without such obedience, it is said, there would be anarchy. Appeal, as one would expect, is typically made to the portion of the ROMANS text which speaks of rulers as a terror to bad conduct. The First Letter of Paul to Timothy is invoked in the same vein: "First of all, then, I urge that supplications, prayers, intercessions, and thanksgivings be made for all men, for kings and all who are in high positions, that we may lead a quiet and peaceable life, godly and respectful in every way" (1 Tim. 2:1–2). Titus is sometimes similarly cited (Tit. 3:1–2).

In practice, this support for the anti-anarchy brief for political obedience has often been adorned to the extent of suggesting that the order enforced by a political regime not only estops or punishes crime or other "bad conduct" but diminishes or minimizes sin. That seems to have been a consideration influential upon Luther where he can be found —paradoxically—requiring obedience for the sake of order even in circumstances where that means endurance of governments deemed wicked.

A crucial factor in citing the biblical passages in First Timothy or Titus or Romans to ground the case for obedience because order is sanctioned by political authority is how far these texts may be thought of as prudential at the time they were written. If they were prompted by a pastoral concern for those living under persecution, or the threat of it or comparable endangerment, then their import is significantly affected where these conditions or risks do not exist. It appears somewhat anomalous, thus, for this argument, concerning order as the reason for obedience to the powers that be, to attain the prominence it has *after* the Constantinian accommodation with its reputed foreclosure of the era of persecution of the early church.

Jonathan Mayhew dealt with these issues and some of his remarks conceive the legitimacy of political authority and, therefore, the terms of obedience to civil rulers, to turn upon the guardianship of the public peace or order, as well as the doing of justice. He, whether wittingly or not, offers a vehement, if belated, answer to Martin Luther's apparent condonation of oppressive regimes:

> If it be our duty, for example, to obey our king merely for this reason, that he rules for the public welfare (which is the only argument the apostle

makes use of), it follows, by a parity of reason, that when he turns tyrant and makes his subjects his prey to devour and destroy, instead of his charge to defend and cherish, we are bound to throw off our allegiance to him, and to resist, and that according to the tenor of the apostle's argument in this passage. Not to discontinue allegiance in this case would be to join with the sovereign in promoting the slavery and misery of that society . . .

For a nation thus abused to arise unanimously and resist their prince, even to the dethroning of him, is not criminal, but a reasonable way of vindicating their liberties and just rights. . . . And it would be highly criminal in them not to make use of this means. It would be stupid tameness and unaccountable folly for whole nations to suffer one unreasonable, ambitious and cruel man to wanton and riot in their misery. And in such a case, it would, of the two, be more rational to suppose that they that did not resist, than they who did, would receive to themselves damnation.

The implication of Mayhew's stand is that as justice is determinative of legitimacy in political authority it is also definitive of order. A tyranny or unjust and illegitimate regime is in itself a form of disorder politically. One is bound to notice, however, that even as the attribution to Luther of tolerance of oppressive or wicked government for the sake of order is paradoxical, so also paradox of equivalent magnitude is evident in Mayhew, since he advocated revolution, with such disorder as revolution occasions, to dethrone or overthrow rulers deemed unjust.

The anomalies and ironies multiply profusely in the many variations which have been propounded to extend the case for submission to the ruling powers because they prevent anarchy, or deter crime, or somehow minimize sin. Perhaps the most elaborate extension, which has had very many adaptations through the centuries since the Constantinian Arrangement, is that which supports incumbent government because a supposed absence of anarchy, which political authority obtains, enables the church to implement its mission. A classical formulation of this, which still survives in the British monarchy, styles the head of state as "defender of the faith". The basic reciprocity, by which the church submits to political authority in its realm while political authority supports or protects the church in its sphere, was subject to numerous forms of political organization and ecclesiastical establishment in colonial America, to recall another place and period where it has had prominence. The later constitutional separation of church and state in the United States, despite its ostensible religious neutrality, and its restraint upon political interference with churches, is more accurately admitted to involve the same kind of reciprocity, save that instead of according legal establishment to a particular church it renders a de facto pluralistic establishment of many churches and sects.

It has proved, over and over, to be but a short step from the notion of political authority to which allegiance is given because that offers a sufficient or necessary order in society for the church to pursue its mission to the idea that the church's own function, through its visible presence and its indoctrination of people, and, sometimes, in its pretention of being the surrogate of God, is to furnish societal stability or to instill complaisance and to teach compliance for the political regime. It was—to mention another instance at point—this version of the anti-anarchy argument which elicited so much sympathy among ecclesiastics and church people for the Nazi cause when it came to power in Germany. (I recommend Arthur Cochrane's *The Church's Confession Under Hitler,* Westminster Press, 1957.)

Political Authority and Empirical Anarchy

The rationale for submission to political authority as a duty of Christians because the state as such, or a specific regime, is said to guarantee a rudimentary or minimal or provisional order in society—controlling crime or, even, restraining sin, and, sometimes, also considered as facilitating or abetting the mission of the church—falls short of being persuasive because it is so historically conditioned. Admittedly, the argument has the aura of tradition, especially that which has accrued during the Constantinian era, but as a general rubric to inform and determine the stance of Christians toward political authority, it is burdened with such relativity as to be more a source of apostasy, indulgence, and mischief most solemn than of anything else. To remain within examples or allusions already cited, this position sanctioned endurance of the rule of George III, but, at the same time, justified the overthrow of that same regime. Or, if it has supplied a basis for civil allegiance to the government of the United States, it must promptly be recalled that it was readily invoked on behalf of the Nazi party and administration in Germany. Such ambivalence is not exceptional with respect to the long history and multifarious adaptations of this proposition, but is redundant. In Luther's time, while it was employed to encourage the rebellion of the German princes against the emperor—and the papacy—it was nevertheless applied to suppress the peasants' revolt against the princes.

Beyond all this, however, is a more theologically significant factor which seems often to be overlooked, notably when discussion of the relation of political authority to the maintenance of social order is pursued on an abstract or pseudo-doctrinal level. If sponsoring order in society be the grounds for obedience to rulers and regimes, then it must be demonstrable that political authority does in fact achieve functional order. It must be, on occasion, evident in an empirical sense that political authority has the capability of establishing order or of preventing anarchy. Let it be noticed, parenthetically, that the term *anarchy* is being used throughout this book in a generic sense and not in the technical meaning the word has in political science as a theory and system which projects an ideal society without organized government—a view, radical only in its naïveté, which lately returns to vogue among younger Americans most disenchanted with the "system". By *anarchy,* I refer to disorder, dysfunction, chaos, confusion of elemental—indeed, primordial—dimension.

Jonathan Mayhew, among others, made the essential observation regarding the association of political authority and empirical anarchy in his conclusion that tyranny represents social disorder, but that insight has elaborate and detailed amplification as one scrutinizes different political systems and administrations. If there is any singular feature among the diversities in governments in the course of many centuries it is that the so-called order which political authority obtains has reference to the enforced preservation of a status quo or to the entrenchment of incumbent regimes or rulers. Within such "order"—quite as commonly—disorder reigns.

Look at America now. The experience, from a human point of view, is one of intense, unremitting, ruthless tumult, strife, and violence. The empirical reality is not order but anarchy:

> Thus, if order in society be the value of government, the most notorious fact about contemporary America is official lawlessness evidenced not only in the criminality, knavery, fraudulent enterprise, illegal and unauthorized conduct of persons in public office—conspicuous in presidents and attorneys general and secretaries of state as well as in the lower echelons of politics—but also in the unconstitutional, unaccountable, outlaw and often conspiratorial operation of the ruling institutions —like the CIA or the FBI or the Pentagon or, for that matter, the Department of Agriculture or the Post Office or the Internal Revenue Service.

> Lawless authority, which in the American experience, has always furnished the effectual rule over blacks and Indians, and some others, is now exposed as endemic in the paramilitarization and covert deployment of the police power throughout society, and in official procurement of crime, accompanied, as it is, by a relentless, caustic, pervasive ridicule of constitutional rights and safeguards and of the rule of law per se as obstructive or inconvenient to police efficiency.

Yet there exists no substantial proof of police effectuality in prosaic law enforcement, in the control of conventional (i.e., unofficial) crime among any classes of the population and in either urban or suburban jurisdictions. More than that, the documentation from police and administrative sources shows, if anything, radical dysfunction in police work, in court administration and in the penal system.

Meanwhile, on other, but related fronts, technocracy facilitates an inversion and debasement of language so that it becomes unsuited for education or other human communication and is instead utilized to manipulate, condition, program, coerce, propagandize, and orchestrate human life. Persons are left isolated, bereft, and vulnerable in a societal and cultural environment congested with jargon, falsehood, euphemism, deception, incoherence, fantasy, and other babel.

In an economy based upon twin policies of indefinite consumption and interminable war or commerce of war, there is gross overdependence upon overproduction of those goods and services, weapons and systems which are least needed or least useful to human beings or which pose the most harmful or fatal potential for human life.

Still, employability is contingent upon this overkill capability in both consumption and war and, together with the operation of a credit structure so fragile, so speculative but so accessible that it achieves impoverishment or indebted dependency for practically everybody who is employed. This victimizes and enslaves human beings by its determination of terms of mere survival which are, at once, most profligate and most meager.

Furthermore, the environment is corrupted and polluted; the means of transportation work spasmodically and are anyway geared to the convenience of computers; waste dominates the depletion of resources; bureaucratic routine has preemptive priority over human need; institutional survival dominates social policy, while the so-called national security is asserted to consist of "a balance of terror".

And, political authority, either in the sense of the "system" or in that of a particular administration, is repeatedly exposed as impotent amidst disorder so ubiquitous.

I believe these to be realistic observations, as to the condition of contemporary America. If the achievement of order be counted the virtue of government and, in turn, the condition precedent for Christian obedience to political authority, I am impelled by the overwhelming evidence of the absence of order now in America, to conclude the prerequisite fails. The appropriate terms to characterize the American scene today, are not those of stability or peace or the rule of law or order, but those of disorder, lawlessness, anarchy or chaos.

If that conclusion is empirically verified, then it underscores the suggestion mentioned earlier that the connotation of order in the traditional argument for submission to the powers that be truly is the satisfaction of the status quo.

It is critical, of course, to the position I affirm here, both politically and theologically, that the present American chaos is *not* novel—not wrought by the impact of advanced technology, not occasioned by thermonuclear overkill, not peculiar to America's imperial grandeur, not simply accountable within American historical circumstances. The disorder in America now represents none other than a particular version of the essential disarray of fallen creation. The empirical description of the American situation is in truth, a specific recital of the biblical story of the fall: of the undoing of creation; of the rupture of all relationships; of the usurpation of the place and integrity of principalities and persons and all created things; of the pervasive incidence of violence; of the loss of vocation; of the consignment of the whole of creation to the active power of death in this age.

If the chaotic reality of contemporary American society corresponds to the havoc of fallen creation, and is not introduced by the emergence of an advanced technocratic state in the United States, and if it is only incidental to and coincidental with the particular prevailing regime, then one can look, as it were, backward and discern the same elemental disorder in *any* society and its political system, while to look forward would offer no essentially different perception of expectancy. Nostalgia does not relieve or alter the insight because there have been no pristine episodes of nations exempted from the fall or spared from captivation with the power and purpose of death at work in history. That is signified in the New Testament witness by the blunt identification of the power of death, incarnate as the devil, as the ruler of the nations and principalities in the temptation of Christ in the wilderness. By the same token, idealism concerning the future of this age which motivates revolutionary causes can not diminish or curtail fallen creation but would only displace one status quo with another, perhaps redistributing victims in the process, but without dislodging the reign of death. On this point, theologically, there is very little distinction to be made between those who long to reestablish an old status quo and so indulge nostalgic sentiments, and those who aspire for a new status quo and so become revolutionary idealists or ideologues. As to either, the biblical witness apprehends them in the same way as an incumbent regime, that is, in terms of the disordering of the life of the whole of creation during the epoch of the fall.

The Scope of Human Sin

Do not confuse this steadfastness of the biblical witness toward political authority, past, present or prospective, with indifference to the oppressions of particular systems or administrations, or with oversight of any other distinctions which may have significance as among various actual and various possible regimes, or with aloofness to empirical needs for change—including change of revolutionary magnitude. The coherence of the biblical apprehension of political authority does not imply any of these but exactly the contrary. But that same coherence is first of all insistent upon confronting and exposing the fullness, the awesomeness, the pervasiveness, the versatility, and the militancy of death's reign in history.

The incredulity of professed Christians, in America especially, concerning the veracity of the biblical story of fallen creation and the consignment of this age to the claim of death as a description of the empirical reality of this world's existence seems, however, to be incorrigible. It adapts many positions or examples, from individualist pietists concentrating sullenly upon a pathetic supposed private justification to social activists pursuing vainly some political ideology assumed to be implicit in the gospel and applicable to the salvation of this world. I do not enter here, an analytical refutation of any of these several aberrant views since this book as a whole is a confessional statement which stands in critique of them. However, in this same connection, it is necessary to notice a basic differentia, as between my own comprehension and that of many others, as to the significance of the fallenness of human life and that of the principalities, including political authority or other ruling institutions.

Put boldly, that issue concerns whether, in the fall, human sin—or the human rejection of life as a gift of the Word of God—is preeminent, and whether, therefore, the fallenness of the nations and other institutions, and the rest of creation, is contingent upon and derivative from human sin. The attribution of such an extraordinary efficacy to sin in human life is to be found in the preaching of Billy Graham as well as in the thought of Reinhold Niebuhr, though rendered in quite different syntax, and even though portending utterly contrary political consequences. My own present understanding, in distinction from both Graham and Niebuhr, is that the fall implicates the whole of creation, not human life alone and not human beings uniquely, and, further, that each and every creature or created thing suffers fallenness in its own right. Thus, to speak concretely, when the chaos of political authority is evident as, say, it is in the existence and dysfunction of the Pentagon technocracy, that constitutes a sign of the fallenness of the principality as such rather than merely the consequence of human depravity or frailty or corruption, either on the part of certain sinful individuals located on the premises of the Pentagon (as Graham might assert) or ascribed to accrued, collective human sin (as Neibuhr argued).

What is at stake—theologically—in this distinction is whether creation belongs to the Word of God as a unique activity. What is at issue—politically—is the scope of human capability vis à vis the principalities and powers which rule this passing age.

As to the theological issue, I suggest that the biblical witness affirms the origination of all of life and of each and every species of life in the Word of God so that the creaturehood of human beings and the creaturely status of nations, institutions and similar beings is, in each case and kind, autonomous one from the other, though none be autonomous from God. In a word, human beings do *not* create institutions or nations or political systems or the like, nor are the same merely projections of aggregated human ideas and actions. These are, biblically speaking, creatures with their own names, identities, integrity, capabilities, proclivities, and, as has been earlier emphasized, vocations. In the fall, all of that is rejected and ruined, so that the principalities exist chaotically and violently, but, at the same time, all that pertains to creaturely integrity is not revoked but is retained in the very Word of God which originates creation.

The same is true, in parallel, I confess so far as human beings are concerned. The confusion attaches to the significance of the dominion bestowed upon human life over the rest of creation, specifically over the principalities and powers. I understand the biblical testament to be that dominion is governance, which, in terms of the creaturely vocations is expressed in the worship of God, in eucharist for the Word of God, in celebration of life as gift. Those who propose that human beings create institutions would embellish dominion to encompass the human authorship of life for such creatures. That same vanity is, alternately, expressed, when the story of the fall is mentioned, in attributing the havoc and disorder of institutions to the lost or spoiled dominion of humans or to human sin. I do not, at all, diminish the potency of sin in human life, I only admonish that human beings should not be so boastful about it, inflating the effectiveness of their sin so as to account for the alienation of the rest of creation and thence belittle the vocation of the Word of God.

This is, I believe, a much needed caution because it directly affects how the restored dominion of human life, exemplified in history in the Lordship of Jesus Christ, is comprehended and enacted. If Christians forswear invidious pretensions about the preeminence of human life in creation, and if they forbear vainglorious constructions of human sin operative in the fall, then they can be renewed in sanity and conscience, in realism and hope, in wholeness and patience as a biblical community in the time being. Otherwise, as has been abundantly and redundantly evidenced in both traditional pietism and conventional activitism, Christians will endure the ignominy of trying to justify themselves or the consternation of attempts to save the world.

So, the differing assessments of the scope of human sin do not represent a fastidious concern. The view I uphold, as distinguished from that of others, confesses how the chaotic situation in contemporary American society is a recitation of the story of the fall rather than a peculiar condition of late American history. The fall means anarchy in creation. That *is* the biblical description: that *is* the empirical reality, whether one assays the present, realistically recalls the past, or beholds the future without fantasy. After all, war *is* chaos; hunger *is* disorganization; pollution *is* havoc; disease *is* dysfunction; tyranny *is* anarchism; violence *is* disorder. Creation is *truly* fallen.

If this elemental manner of speaking of the profound moral confusion in which fallen political authority thrives sounds apocalyptic, so be it! The Apocalypse designates the end of this perishing age, the last calamity of the rulers of the world, the utter destruction of systems and regimes of political authority, the categorical devastation of the reign of death, the finale of time. But Doomsday is imminent as well as ultimate. So long as time lasts the apocalyptic reality impends upon each and every happening; in the very anarchy and futility that mark the fallen principalities and powers empirically the Apocalypse is forecast and portended.

Bombast and Blasphemy

A reason that I find the traditional bases for Christian submission to the powers that be so deeply unsatisfactory is that those arguments assessing the legitimacy of political authority or those asserting that political authority provides order and prevents anarchy are confounded or refuted empirically. Yet it is the correspondence between biblical faith and empirical reality—or to say it somewhat differently—discernment of the militancy of the Word of God incarnate in common history—which is the genius of the biblical witness. It is, to my mind, not so much that the ideas about legitimacy or order are false, in a dogmatic sense, but that they are too abstract, too small or too narrow to accommodate the gospel, too convenient to emperors and officials, too simplistic and too misleading for the faithful. I am unable to circumvent, for example, the incongruity of Luther's tolerance of tyranny because that saves order when the order which is enforced, in fact, is disorder. At the same time, when Mayhew pronounces a tyrannical regime illegitimate and unworthy of obedience, I respond more sympathetically to Mayhew than to Luther, but I still cannot abide the resort to violence which Mayhew would advocate to overthrow the illegitimate regime because that also is basically incongruous.

In the turbulent and ambiguous history of Christendom, especially under the auspices of the Constantinian Arrangement, such difficulties as these have been immeasurably more complicated and aggravated by elaborate sophistry constructing pernicious doctrines, categorically alien to biblical faith, propounding "just wars" or premising "Christian nations". (Solemn treatises on both of these topics, transposed largely into the argot of the Pentagon, can be found in the *Annual Defense Department Report,* FY 1976 and FY 197T. The report uses, or abuses, Luke 11:21 as a theme.) The genocide, mayhem, tortures, imprisonments, inquisitions, persecutions, repressions and variegated injustices instigated and rationalized by these sophisms are, by now, literally incalculable. The penultimate event in this horrendous legacy of Christendom is—let every Christian confess —the Holocaust. If that be true, then the whole premise of obedience to political authority based on order or legitimacy, as that has been pronounced and propagated within the Constantinian ethos, identified by pseudo-doctrines of "just war" or of "Christian nation," is exposed as ridiculous.

The outrage of the Holocaust was atrocious and traumatic enough for humanity so that some sense of a duty to disobey political authority was articulated in a worldly way in the Nuremberg Principles recognized in 1946 as a basis for the war crimes trials after World War II. Yet, in the same period of time, and since, the churches in the nations of the West have remained either silent or equivocal, clinging, despite all that has transpired, to the inherited vested interest furnished to the churches in the Contantinian status quo. It is no surprise, then, that these same churches, with but few exceptions, surveyed the genocide in Vietnam obscurely and endured it mutely. And it is equally unsurprising that current versions of these same pernicious doctrines have been regorged both in vulgar bicentennial rites and in solemn shibboleths concerning national security and the sacred destiny of America. The implication of such notions, so offensive to biblical faith, is the imputation that, somehow, the salvation of the world depends upon the asserted moral superiority of America among the nations or, indeed, upon its identification as Zion. Therefore, the overwhelming priority of so-called national security, the licensing of war and genocide, and the deployment of overkill nuclear capability, along with covert operations, recruitment of missionaries as secret agents, assassination plots, and official conspiracies intervening in other nations are accounted justified.

These very matters are essentially treated in REVELATION, which may be enough to explain the widespread neglect which REVELATION has had in the churches. In the 13th chapter, at the verge of the Apocalypse, wherein the nations are portrayed as horrendous predatory beasts, the significant term employed by the author to set forth offense of political authority before the Word of God is *blasphemy*. Not only is blasphemy named repeatedly in REVELATION 13 as the crucial word, but it is so named, frequently, elsewhere in the Book of Revelation.

If blasphemy or "bombast and blasphemy" seem, today, curious symbols to convey the weight which their usage in the texts in REVELATION indicate, it is perhaps because nowadays we seldom think of the occurrence of blasphemy, save where we intend to refer to heavy cursing or obscene utterance. Ron Zeigler, then still the presidential press officer, once excused, during the Watergate episode, the failure of the White House to furnish certain Nixon tapes which had been ordered by Judge John Sirica to be submitted to the court, by stating that the tapes had been delayed in their surrender because of the time required to "delete the blasphemies". I suppose Zeigler meant obscenities, though I would not quarrel that he was, for once at least, telling the whole truth in his remark. In any case, blasphemy means more than obscenity or more than literal cursing, as the term is used in REVELATION. In REVELATION it denotes wanton and contemptuous usurpation of the very vocation of God, villification of the Word of God and persecution of life as life originates in the Word of God, preemptive attempt against the sovereignty of the Word of God in this world, brute aggression against human life which confesses or appeals to the Word of God.

Elsewhere in REVELATION there is some specificity about the blaspheming policy and conduct of political authority— notably trade and war or the features of imperial grandeur are mentioned, the vices commonly attributed to so-called permissive societies are *not* enumerated—but the term of most comprehensive reference, the word that encompasses and implies everything else is blasphemy. Not illegitimacy, not anarchy, not injustice, but blasphemy, so that blasphemy recapitulates and relates these other terms. So where there is illegitimacy in political authority or the disorder of co-erced order, or injustice of any degree afflicted upon anyone, there is blasphemy. And when nations conceive their own sanctification and pronounce wars just, there is the bombast and blasphemy of the Antichrist.

To say the same thing in another way, the biblical witness not only stands against tyranny and oppression as such but comprehends tyranny and oppression as blasphemy, that is, as the repudiation and defamation of the Lordship of Christ in common history by the ruling powers and political prin-cipalities. The offense against humanity which any tyranny or injustice represents is, as it were, escalated because of Christ's dominion over fallen creation, so that it is not merely an offense against specific, conspicuous victims but is a burden for all humanity and for the life of the whole of creation, an aggression against the Word of God in which that life is bestowed, or so that it is exposed as blasphe-mous. It is, hence, not happenstance or sentimentality or, even, compassion that occasions the biblical association of the people of God with the impoverished, dispossessed, im-prisoned, diseased, outcast, but that identification verifies, honors and implements the confession that Jesus Christ *is* Lord.

Today, the Barmen Declaration in which the confessing church in Germany publicly rebuked the demonic reality of political authority in the emerging Nazi state is aptly re-membered as an exemplary witness. The Barmen Declara-tion represents that precisely because it is a confession of the Lordship of Christ and the historic as well as cosmic significance of the Lordship of Christ instead of it having been a political or ideological or religious manifesto. Barmen went far beyond such critique of Nazi politics and policy as any of the latter might make. Barmen means something quite distinguishable: it confessed the gospel. If, to some, nowadays, that seems quaint or irrelevant or beside the point, in a nation confronted with the spectre of Nazi totalitarianism, Hitler and the Nazi party had a more accurate perception of what the Barmen Declaration signified. *They* knew, at the time, in 1934, that Barmen named the Nazi principality as the Antichrist and that that was not only an exposé and rebuke of the Nazi political authority, but an admonishment that the Word of God is active in judgment in this world. It is the warning of Barmen of the impending destruction of the Nazi regime before the Word of God that explicates the fury of the regime in pursuing everyone who subscribed to the confession until every single one of them had been executed or imprisoned or exiled.

chapter four

Besides this you know what hour it is, how it is full time now for you to wake from sleep. For salvation is nearer to us now than when we first believed; the night is far gone, the day is at hand. Let us then cast off the works of darkness and put on the armor of light; let us conduct ourselves becomingly as in the day . . .

Romans 13:11–13a

And authority was given [the beast] over every tribe and people and tongue and nation, and all who dwell on earth will worship it, every one whose name has not been written before the foundation of the world in the book of life of the Lamb that was slain. If any one has an ear, let him hear:

If any one is to be taken captive,
to captivity he goes;
if any one slays with the sword,
with the sword must he be slain.

Here is a call for the endurance and faith of the saints.

Revelation 13:7b–10

The
Second
Advent
of the Lord

The audacity—and the biblical authenticity—of the Barmen witness is that it is the confession that the Word of God is sovereign here and now: that the Word of God is active and efficacious in judgment of the rulers of this passing and perishing age: that Jesus Christ is the Lord.

I emphasize that, in this confession, the Barmen Declaration is exemplary; it is *not* exceptional. That fact has been recognized where Barmen has been treated as a creed and used liturgically, after the manner in which ancient or venerable creeds and confessions are invoked as definitive and essential in the public worship of God in the church.

Such travesty as there may be said to be in the church's public worship, today or in the past, in America or elsewhere, raises the question of whether the participants are ignorant or religiose, but that does not alter the truth confessed that the Word of God is not daunted, detoured, delayed, or diminished by the fall. The power of death vested in political authority, or otherwise, is fearsome, guileful, predatory and, as REVELATION 13 mentions, wondrous, but the power of death is impotent before the Lord./Though political authority persecute those who live now in Christ, it is powerless to captivate them. In short, for biblical peo-ple—in the twentieth century, as Barmen exemplifies, or in the first century, as either ROMANS or REVELATION attest in their respective ways—the issues of conscience and obedience in relation to political authority intrinsically concern the sovereignty of the Word of God in history and within that dominion exercised by Jesus Christ as Lord in this age. That implicates every detail of the life and the death and the resurrection of Jesus, but it involves most bluntly and notoriously his coming into the world and his coming again.

The Significance of the Two Advents

The biblical treatment of both advents, the narratives attending Christ's birth, and the testimonies about the Second Coming of Christ, is manifestly political. Yet, curiously, people have come to hear the story of the birth as apolitical and even as antipolitical, while, I venture, most listen to news of Christ coming again triumphantly with vague uneasiness or even outright embarrassment. What with the star and the sheep and the stable, it has been possible to acculturate the birth, to render it some sort of pastoral idyll. But the scenic wonders, the astonishing visions, the spectacular imagery associated with the next advent have confounded the ordinary processes of secularization and thus the subject of the Second Coming has been either omitted or skimmed in the more conventional churches or else exploited variously by sectarians, charlatans, fanatics or huckster evangelists.

Insofar as these allegations are sound, the mystery of both advents has been dissipated, whereas it is an affirmation of the mystery of both events that is most needed in order to be lucid, at all, about either advent.

So I begin by affirming the mystery of these happenings and, furthermore, by noticing that what can be known of the two advents is no more than that evident in their biblical connection. It is the coherence of one advent in the other advent, the first in the second and, simultaneously the second in the first, that is crucial.

Or, in other words, I do not know if, when Jesus was born, there appeared a special star over Bethlehem, any more than I know whether, when Jesus comes as Judge and King, he will be seen mid-air, descending amidst the clouds. Nor do I have need to know such things, they by no means control my salvation, much less the world's redemption. Yet, since both advents are mysteries, these styles bespeak those mysteries aptly, or so it seems to me.

There is a secret in the first advent, a hidden message in the coming of Jesus Christ into the world, a cryptic aspect in the unfolding of Christmas. Indeed, the biblical accounts of the birth of the child in Bethlehem, in such quaint circumstances, represents virtually a parody of the advent promise.

A similar discreteness—at times of such degree as to be ironical—marked the entire public life of Jesus Christ, according to the Bible. He taught in parables, finishing his stories enigmatically with the remark—*if you have ears that can hear, then hear.* (cf. Matt. 1:1–23.) When he healed a person or freed a demoniac, he admonished witnesses to *see that no one hears about this.* (As in Mark 7:31–37.) When he was accused by the religious and political authorities, and confronted by Pontius Pilate, *he refused to answer one word, to the Governor's great astonishment.* (Mark 15:5.)

The first chapter of the Gospel of St. John tells this mystery in the coming of Jesus Christ: "He was in the world; but the world, though it owed its life to him, did not recognize him. He entered his own realm, and his own would not receive him."

For primitive Christians, so much defamed and so often harassed and sometimes savaged in first century Rome, the secret of the first advent was thought to be in the consolation of the next advent. The pathos and profound absurdity of the birth of Jesus Christ was understood to be trans-

figured in the Second Coming of Jesus Christ. The significance of advent could only be realized in the hope of the
return of Jesus Christ.

It is the Book of Revelation which most eagerly anticipates the Second Coming, and in Revelation one hears a
recurring theme, summed up, for instance, in the 11th chapter at verse 15: "The sovereignty of the world has passed
to our Lord and his Christ, and he shall reign for ever and
ever!"

The same is repeated, again and again and again in Revelation, in the names and titles ascribed to Christ. He is the
ruler of the kings of the earth. He is *the sovereign Lord of
all.* He is *the King of kings.* He is the *judge* of the nations.
He is the One *worthy to receive all power and wealth, wisdom and might, honor and glory and praise!*

All of these are political designations and point to the
truth, from the vantage of the next advent, that the first
advent's secret is political. And that truth becomes evident
in the traditional stories recalled and recited in observance
of the first advent.

Thus, the journey of Joseph and the pregnant Mary took
place in order that they be enrolled for a special tax which
was not simply a source of revenue for the Roman occupy-
ing regime but, as all taxes are, also a means of political
surveillance of potentially dissident people.

And the profound threat which the coming of Christ poses
for mundane rulers is to be seen in Herod's cooption of the
Magi to locate the child so that Herod could slay him.
When the attempt fails, Herod's anxiety becomes so vehement that he slaughters a whole generation of children
in seeking to destroy Christ.

Later, John the Baptist, whose calling as a messenger and
herald is especially remembered in the season of advent,
suffers terrible interrogation and torture, imprisonment and
decapitation because his preparation for the ministry of the
Christ who has come is perceived by the rulers as a most
awesome warning.

Or, again, the manger scene itself is a political portrait of the whole of creation restored in the dominion of Jesus Christ in which every creature, every tongue and tribe, every rule and authority, every nation and principality is reconciled in homage to the Word of God incarnate.

Amidst portents and events such as these, commemorated customarily in the church, the watchword of Christmas— "peace on earth"—is not a sentimental adage but a political utterance and an eschatological proclamation, indeed, a preview and precursor of the Second Coming of Christ the Lord, which exposes the sham and spoils the power of the rulers of the age.

Those first century Christians, pursued and persecuted, scorned and beleagured, as they were because of their insight, were right: the secret of the first advent is the consolation of the second advent. The message in both advents *is* political. It celebrates the assurance that in the coming of Jesus Christ the nations and the rulers of the nations are judged in the Word of God, which is, at the same time, to announce that in the Lordship of Christ they are rendered accountable to human life and to that of the whole of creation.

The Impending Devastation of Political Authority

Each advent of Christ is attended by mystery, what is now known of either event is not all that is to be known, but what is confessed by Christians as to both advents is known to them through the conjunction of the two.

That which is known and affirmed now because of the first advent and in the expectancy of the second advent is, however, enough to be politically decisive, that is to say, enough to edify choice and action in issues of conscience and obedience with respect to the rulers of the world. In the first advent, Christ comes as Lord; in the next advent, Christ the Lord comes as judge of the world and the world's principalities and thrones, in vindication of His reign and of the sovereignty of the Word of God in history. This is the wisdom, which the world deems folly, which biblical people bear and by which they live as the church in the world for the time being.

The message which the life and witness of the church conveys to political authority, hence, always, basically, concerns the political vigilance of the Word of God in judgment. That news is, at once, an admonishment to all earthly rulers that Christ the Lord reigns already, as the first advent signifies, and an anticipation of the destruction of all worldly political authority at the Second Coming.

Judgment—biblically—*does* mean the destruction of the ruling powers and principalities of this age. I am aware that this is, for professed Christians in America and in many other nations, an unthinkable thought even though it be biblical (1 Cor. 15:24–28; cf. Acts 2:34–36, Rev. 18–20).

The Constantinian mentality which afflicts the church equivocates contemplation of the judgment of the Word of God. Within the Constantinian ethos, the church even seeks, in the name of the Word of God, to broker compromises of that judgment with princes and presidents, regimes and systems. The capacity of God for anger is gainsaid, though it be in the face of the chaos—the war and hunger and famine and disease and tyranny and injustice—over which the rulers of this age in truth preside. Nevertheless, the biblical emphasis upon the judgment cannot be omitted or denied, including those references, most disconcerting to emperors and their like, which render judgment vehemently, as the *wrath* of God or as his vengeance or retribution.

More than that, the biblical witness expects that the devastation of political authority is coincident in the judgment with the fulfillment of political authority. All that political authority signifies in fallen creation, in consignment to the power of death, has its consummation and perfection in the vindication of the reign of Christ. The rule of the powers of this age, which incarnates death and which is futile, is undone and ended in judgment which substantiates Christ's dominion over the whole of creation. The judgment of the Word of God means that ending of time and history which constitutes the restoration of creation, and, within that, the return of political authority to its own vocation as God's servant for the benefit of human life.

Christians rejoice, on behalf of all humanity and, indeed, all creation, at the prospect of the judgment because in that Last Day the destruction of political authority at once signals its consummation in the kingdom of God.

The Imminence of the Second Advent

The rejoicing is constant, the anticipation is eager, the eschatological expectation is imminent. While—as has been said—the apocalyptic reality impends in any moment in any event in the diffusion of this age, so, simultaneously, the eschatological truth is represented in any moment in any event in this world, to those whose eyes see and whose ears hear.

I believe that the gifts of discernment are undiminished today as compared to the day of the apostles; indeed, I regard discernment as still definitive of faith as well as witness. Yet I am aware that the discerning gifts are much scorned and often neglected in the contemporary church. That is significantly evident in the absence now of the sense of eschatological imminence which, the New Testament reports, so agitated the apostolic Christians. In turn, insofar as that imminent expectancy of the Second Coming of the Lord has been lost, the Christian witness vis-à-vis the powers that be has been disconcerted, and the rejoicing has been greatly inhibited. But I consider that the second advent *is* imminent and that Christians in the twentieth century may, and should, regard it with as much passion and excitement as did those of the first century.

While saying this, I know that the prevailing view, chiefly sponsored by church historians, is different. The usual construction nowadays is that the first Christians expected the coming of Christ, in glory, promptly, and that this expectation lapsed as time continued, necessitating, eventually, drastic revisions in eschatology, if not its suppression altogether.

In just this connection, the Constantinian comity is, once again, pertinent because the loss of the conviction about the imminence of the Eschaton so readily abets the dependency of the church upon the political powers and other institutions of the status quo, in place of a *raison d'etre* of the church as the historic pioneer of the kingdom of God. From there the descent is quick and facile into the sophistries about "Christian nations" and into pagan idealism which distorts the biblical precedent of the church. At the same time, in counterpoint, there have come and gone in Christendom assorted sects assembled by fundamentalist or sorcerous calculations purporting to fix the hour of Christ's return.

I conclude that both forecasters and scholastic revisionists misconstrue the meaning of eschatological imminence.

Because time inheres in the reality of death and because the Kingdom destroys death's reign and abolishes time, to think and speak, at all, of the coming of the Kingdom must comprehend the significance of the ending of time. At the outset, it must be realized, thought and speech are taxed because both remain confined in time. The entire vocabulary in human usage is temporal. To employ any of it to attempt to elucidate the finale of time is an extraordinary, and incongruous, effort in which words can never mean simply what they say.

Recognizing that much cautions against any simplistic literalism or any merely historically conditioned interpretations and prays for a more mature and profound communication in which the words, uttered in time, are sacramentalized or transfigured, and that fittingly, since the topic is the Eschaton.

Characteristically, the biblical witness, in Scripture as such and in the life of the church, speaks in marvelously versatile and appropriately diverse ways of the second advent: prophetically, metaphorically, parabolically, ecstatically, sacramentally, dogmatically, poetically, narratively— in every tongue or style or syntax or idiom available. The biblical witness speaks, thus, multifariously of the coming of the King and his kingdom to show that the subject is inexhaustible and one which truly exceeds the capabilities of human speech.

This is an aspect of the sense of imminence biblical people have concerning the Kingdom. More than that imminence expresses eternal reality in time, a way of representing how the eschatological is freed from time, or of bespeaking the ending of time before time has ended. The relationship, in other words, between the Word of God and creation, even in time, transcends time and is, from a human point of view, imminent at any time. In the Word of God a thousand years are not more than a moment.

If some have put aside the expectation, it is not because Christ is tardy and not because God has postponed the next advent, but because the consciousness of imminence has been confused or lost. I regard the situation of contemporary Christians as much the same as that of our early predecessors in the faith so far as anticipation of the Second Coming matters. We expect the event at any moment. We hope for it in every moment. We live in the imminence of the Eschaton. That is the only way, for the time being, to live humanly.

The conviction of eschatological imminence which informs the witness of biblical people during this passing age is grounded in the insight they bear, on behalf of the life of the world, into the political secret of the first advent, which also inheres in creation itself in spite of the fall, that is, the Lordship of Christ. Knowledge of the truth hidden in the first advent, confession of Christ as Lord, means recognition of the sovereignty of the Word of God acting in history to restore dominion to humanity in creation. The anticipation of the second advent is for the consummation of Christ's reign as Lord so that what is secret becomes notorious, what is revealed is transfigured triumphantly, what is witnessed biblically is publicly vindicated.

In the dispensation between (as it were) the two advents, which is no more than a moment for the Word of God or in the expectation of the people of God, the task of Christians is shaped by the imminent, constantly impinging, eschatological hope. And, as I was saying, it is this which becomes crucial in decisions and actions of conscience and obedience in nation and in church, rather than, as is so vainly and persistently supposed, the operation of some great principle. The ethics of biblical people concerns events not moral propositions. And if to the world, to fellow citizens of some nation or to the ruling powers, the way of the biblical witness seems enigmatic, inconsistent, sometimes apparently contradictory, suspect, foolish, then so be it. Christians do not covet anyone's approval or applause, least of all do they seek or envy the sanction of governments. The Christian life has its only—and its only possible—explication in the judgment of the Word of God.

So biblical people live patiently, awaiting the coming of the Lord, in the midst of death's feigned rule over fallen creation, discerning pervasive portents of the impending devastation while beholding profuse signs of the redemption of fallen creation. To live, thus, in hope, or to live by grace, or to confess the vitality of the judgment of the Word of God in history: all these mean the same thing.

Evidently, many of the people of the churches do not participate in this hope which trusts the judgment, but are enticed by futile hopes or entrapped in false hopes which betray a witness that is conformed and doomed. These are plethora, and I make no effort to enumerate or refute them here, except to notice that they commonly signify a particular misapprehension of the gospel, a specific confusion expressing bewilderment about the promise of Christ's second advent and skepticism about the veracity of Christ's resurrection. It is, typically, a witness which acts as if the triumph of the Word of God over the power of death in this world had not been enacted and verified in the resurrection of Christ but remains, somehow, incomplete or inconclusive so that the task assigned to Christians is to finish or achieve that victory. What issues, in consequence, is an expectancy that the Kingdom marks such a success. In this manner *the perfection of the resurrection is actually substituted for the coming of Christ as Judge and King!* If there be subtlety in this transposition, there is nothing subtle about its implications: it ignores the political secret of the first advent while it radically diminishes the office of God in judgment of the world; it denies the efficacy of the resurrection in demonstrating the accessibility, here and now, of the Word of God enabling human life to transcend the fear and thrall of death, while it distorts and inflates the calling of Christians and the mission of the church in this age. It may occasion, variously, the cooption of popular ideology or of transient revolutionary causes or of programs for political and social reform or idealism but is just as adapted to stupid allegiance to the powers that be. And these, or any of these, are then misnamed for the gospel. Curiously, though it vainly aspires to conquer death, being reluctant to believe the resurrection of Christ, it actually, fatally, underestimates the wiles of the power of death. It succumbs to exactly the temptations which Jesus refuted in the wilderness.

If there is no resurrection from death, Christians are to be pited (cf. 1 Cor. 15:14.) If Christ is not raised, the faith is in vain. If, by virtue of Christ's resurrection, human beings are not offered freedom now from bondage to death in this world, then there is no hope worthy of human belief at all. "But in fact Christ has been raised from the dead" (1 Cor. 15:20a). Christians are those human beings who live now within the efficacy of His resurrection. And in their peculiar witness to the power of the resurrection, Christians eagerly expect and patiently await the Second Coming of Jesus Christ, with a glad and trustworthy knowledge that what is vindicated in the judgment is the Lordship of Christ, *not* the Christians since they are also judged by the Word of God.

chapter five

For the same reason you also pay taxes, for the authorities are ministers of God, attending to this very thing. Pay all of them their dues, taxes to whom taxes are due, revenue to whom revenue is due, respect to whom respect is due, honor to whom honor is due.
Owe no one anything, except to love one another; for he who loves his neighbor has fulfilled the law.

Romans 13:6–8

And it was allowed to give breath to the image of the beast so that the image of the beast should even speak, and to cause those who will not worship the image of the beast to be slain. Also it causes all, both small and great, both rich and poor, both free and slave, to be marked on the right hand or the forehead, so that no one can buy or sell unless he has the mark, that is, the name of the beast or the number of its name.

Revelation 13:15–17

chapter five

The
Vocation
of the Church
as the Holy Nation

The frequent confusion in the church by which the significance of Christ's resurrection is imputed to the Second Coming of Christ accounts for the depletion of the consciousness of the imminence of eschatological reality.

The matter is not one of theological nicety because it has extensive consequences for the practical scope of the witness offered by the church. Not the least of these is the belittlement of the judgment of the Word of God by the political rulers of this age. If one does not esteem the resurrection as the decisive reason for acknowledging the sovereignty of the Word of God in history, then judgment as an activity of God is virtually disassociated from the affairs of political authority in this world. If one supposes that, somehow, the resurrection is inconclusive over the power of death or is yet to be completed, or, more scandalous from a biblical vantage, that the Christian task in the world is, somehow, to complete the resurrection, then the Lordship of Christ, signifying the reign of the Word of God in history which is consummated on the Last Day in the destruction and fulfillment of all political authority, is derogated to dependency upon the prestige of the church. That is soft ground, indeed, upon which to confront the ruling principalities. In other words, where this extraordinary confusion thrives, the rudimentary biblical concern about political authority, expressed in the REVELATION passages on the bombast and blasphemy of the beast, for the affirmation now of the sovereignty of the Word of God and for the vindication of that sovereignty in the judgment, is discarded.

While I forebear comment about the ineptness and essential aburdity of Christians, or the church, struggling to do what God has already done in the resurrection of Christ, I cannot omit how the confusion mentioned sidesteps or undercuts the vocational issue, earlier discussed in this book, and how that affects what Christians, or the church, say and do with respect to political authority. Whether, in any particular situation, Christians, or the church, are found to be opposing or supporting a political regime or system, the biblical authority for the attitude and action is the vocation of political authority, as well as all other creatures, in the worship of God: The vocation is to be, as ROMANS says, "the servants of God" for the sake of the life of the whole creation. Whether, specifically, in praise or rebuke, in adherence or admonishment, Christians are engaged in recalling political authority to its vocation—and that, incessantly, until, in the coming again of Christ, that vocation is restored to political authority and the whole of fallen creation knows redemption.

Manifestly, these considerations bear upon how the several famous "honor" passages in the New Testament are read, including the remark of Jesus, "Then render to Caesar the things that are Caesar's, and to God the things that are God's" (Luke 20:25; cf. Luke 23:2).

With the Constantinian mentality so prevalent, it is common to recite these texts as pithy aphorisms with an *a priori* assumption that there is necessarily *something* due Caesar whatever the circumstances. I do not find any such assumption automatically justified, and moreover I believe any aphoristic recitations from the Bible to be an abuse of the biblical witness. Withal, none of the texts cited furnish rationale for uncritical submission to the demands for tribute by political authority. REVELATION emphasizes this most caustically by indicating that those who bear not the mark of the beast will be slain by the beast. First Peter enjoins honor for the sovereign—as distinguished from an incumbent officeholder—and, moreover, places that in contingency to three other actions: *Honor all men; Love the brotherhood; Fear God;* the last of which is a very direct reference to the judgment.

In ROMANS, the comparable text is most redundant on the matter of what is due, rather than what political authority may command or coerce, and what is appropriately due is related to the vocation of political authority as ordained or instituted by God or as a minister or servant of God.

When the ROMANS passage is falsely or carelessly invoked aphoristically, the preceding heavy allusion to the judgment is overlooked, as is the ensuing commentary on the importance of the imminence of the next advent.

Trusting the Judgment of the Word of God

The passages proximate to ROMANS 13:1–7 are, nonetheless, commonly suppressed while attention is fixed upon the seven famous verses. I have already indicated that I regard that oversight of the immediate context an exploitation of ROMANS 13:1–7, particularly where it is self-serving to emperors and officials, but it then becomes necessary to inquire about the impact of the adjacent passages which furnish the setting for the first seven verses of ROMANS 13. What is the significance of ROMANS 12 and, then, the remainder of ROMANS 13 for ROMANS 13:1–7?

One conceivable response is to read the seven verses as stating a duty of submission, in a relatively straightforward fashion, as prudential counsel for the faithful. This is an approach of some popularity, especially among those who think that Paul was, here, seeking a positive relationship with political authority which would obviate or forestall official hostility toward the Christians. Sometimes this is joined, in relation to the attending texts, with a chronological eschatology, attributed to Paul, which rationalizes indifference to political matters and to the conditions of this world in general. The difficulty with this device is that it asserts too broad an inference, based upon the remaining verses of chapter 13, but one which does not find support in chapter 12, or, for that matter, elsewhere in the writings of Paul or the news of Paul's energetic ministry. Yet if Paul cannot be said to rationalize indifference to this world, and to its ruling powers, are the texts in chapter 12 and in chapter 13 altogether to be heard as prudential counsel, so that ROMANS 13:1–7 is not some interpolation or intrusion or interruption? That way offers no help either, as far as I can see, because it renders the passages adjacent to the seven verses largely nonsensical as advice for safe conduct in this world. *Do not be conformed to this world*—that is no prudence (Rom. 12:2a). *Bless those who persecute you*— bah!—the wisdom of the world is "appease those who persecute you" (Rom. 12:14a). Or, again, in ROMANS 12:16: *associate with the lowly; never be conceited.* Where *would* the church, as we know it, be if it practiced such advice? In short, the way to construe the seven verses of chapter 13 as prudential counsel *is* by exempting them from their context in the Letter.

An alternative is to treat the seven verses about political authority in their context in the Letter and affirm the eschatological orientation of the whole of chapters 12 and 13. If that be the effort not only do the appeals of Paul not to be conformed to this world, but transformed, or his mention of the use of the charismatic gifts, or his exhorting unconditioned love, or his insistence that judgment is God's prerogative, or his focus on conduct "becomingly as in the day" have coherence, but the particular mention of obedience to rulers retains connection with the sovereignty of the Word of God, with the imminence of the judgment, and with the vocation of political authority.

Or, to put the same view in terms of *bless those who persecute you; bless and do not curse them,* how does one bless, and not curse, the predatory monster save by the freedom, warranted, as the passage goes on to declare, by the judgment, in which God's sovereignty is vindicated, to recall political authority to its vocation as the servant or minister of God?

Furthermore, if, as REVELATION reminds, the consequence of so blessing political authority is *to be slain*, the character of this freedom to *bless those who persecute you* as trust in the judgment is all the more cogent.

Well, to bring the matter to the present, that is just as much the truth about the Barmen Declaration.

It is the critical relationship of the expectation of the judgment, held in a sense of imminence by the biblical community, to fallen political authority that prompts me to search for another way of dealing with issues of conscience and obedience than that traditionally furnished by the rubrics of legitimacy or order. My rejection of these customary criteria is, I reiterate, not so much out of a conclusion that they are false as that they are biblically inappropriate and, in some of their versions, misleading. They fail to take sufficiently into account the stories of creation and fall, they minimize or sometimes ignore the vocational issue as it emerges from those stories, they are too abstract, too arbitrary, too artificial, too narrow, they have become far too conditioned by the Constantinian environment and too convenient to its comity favoring the status quo. They fail to be empirically realistic, they are often associated with profound misapprehension of the resurrection and, therefore, about the witness given to the church in the time being, and about the active hope of Christians for the consummation of history in which the sovereignty of the Word of God, which enables the biblical lifestyle now, is triumphantly substantiated.

By the same token, the attempt to articulate an alternative to the traditional considerations of legitimacy or order, must not indulge empirical realism so much that it depresses or immobilizes the witness of the church; it must be wary of becoming secretly idolatrous of the power of death just becauses death *is* so awesome, prevasive, and versatile in fallen creation; it must not assume because the Constantinian mentality, by now so deeply inbred in Christendom, turns upside down the precedent of the apostolic church that it daunts the Holy Spirit at work in either the church or the world; and, thus, it must not countenance or encourage, even inadvertently, sentiments of apathy, withdrawal, complaisance, or indifference in Christians in the world.

The Biblical Witness as Advocacy

A clue, to me most edifying, is the advocacy characteristic of the New Testament. This clue is evident in every episode in the Gospels in which Jesus ministers to the despised, the diseased, the dispossessed or in which he confronts the rich, the powerful, the mighty. (e.g. Matt. 8:5–10 and 9:10–13; Mark 5:35–43; Luke 16:19–31; John 4:46–54.)

It is verified in the comparable Acts of the Apostles. (Acts 3:1–4:31)

It is redundant in the exhortations of Paul's epistles. (Notably in the Corinthian Correspondence.)

It is confirmed in the letters of other authors. (As in the Letter of James or the First Letter of John.)

It is a strenuous emphasis in the Book of Revelation (Rev. 21 and 22).

In the resurrection, this is epitomized wherein Christ serves as advocate of all humanity throughout time (cf. Acts 17:29–31; Rom. 31–39).

So, in this age the church of Christ is called as the advocate of every victim of the rulers of the age, and that, not because the victim is right, for the church does not know how any are judged in the Word of God, but because the victim is a victim.

Advocacy is how the church puts into practice its own experience of the victory of the Word of God over the power of death, how the church lives in the efficacy of the resurrection amidst the reign of death in this world, how the church expends its life in freedom from both intimidation and enthrallment of death or of any agencies of death, how the church honors the sovereignty of the Word of God in history against the counterclaims of the ruling principalities. This advocacy, in its ecumenical scope as well as its actual specificity, constitutes the church's political task, but, simultaneously, exemplifies the church's worship of God, as intercession for anyone in need, and for the need of the whole of creation, which exposes and confounds the blasphemy of predatory political authority.

I have been hesitant, throughout this book, to offer examples to illustrate or elucidate, though they be readily available, because of the vogue, which I notice ruefully, of reducing examples to models, instead of hearing them as precedents or parables, as if, once so charted, the model could be duplicated or even prefabricated. Still instances may be cited, names may be commended to verify the biblical witness as advocacy as that appears in the life of the church now, as well as in the New Testament, if the caution against the indulgence in modeling and role playing is observed.

In the political crisis in Chile, following upon the usurpation of constitutional government wrought, as Americans belatedly learned, to a great extent by lawless collusion of the Central Intelligence Agency, the National Security Council, the military establishment and the Nixon presidency, the episcopate of the church, through Raul Cardinal Silva Henriquez, issued a statement. It protested the harsh suppression of civil liberties by the Chilean regime and, significantly, affirmed the task of the church in society in this way: "The Church must be the voice of all, especially of those who do not have a voice." (The *New York Times,* April 25, 1974, p. 12.)

Or, in another instance, there is the well known ministry of Will Campbell as an advocate of the outcast, who was, as a white Mississippian, an early and singular pioneer in the struggle of Southern blacks against racism, and who has

had an extraordinary pastoral ministry among folk of the
Ku Klux Klan since they became despised and lowly.

Meanwhile, for nearly half a century, the exemplary effort
of Dorothy Day perseveres—literally giving water to those
who thirst, clothing the naked, offering shelter to the deso-
late, caring for those imprisoned. She has, simply, *done* the
twelfth chapter of ROMANS, and, appropriate to that chapter,
in a way which makes her advocacy intercessory—in a
manner which renders it worship.

And there are others, I notice a host of them, dispersed
in characteristic witness. And if there is still temptation to
stereotype the advocacy involved, then observe the mention
in ROMANS of the diversity of gifts distributed throughout
the body of the church in order that no victim be without
an advocate (Rom. 12:6–15).

If the witness of advocacy is considered in explicit relation to political authority, the fragile nature of the familiar
tests for obedience and conscience in terms of legitimacy
and order is exposed. The problem, with respect to the ambiguity of legitimacy, was mentioned in the second chapter
in citing the government established by the American Revolution. For George III, and for assorted Tories, on both
sides of the Atlantic, the new government was illegitimate,
while its legitimacy was asserted as self-evident by the
Founding Fathers and their adherents. But what of those
in America who were victims in various ways of the new
regime—those without franchise or access to public office
because they owned no property, those excluded because
they were female, Indians for whom the change in political
authority, if anything, increased the hazards to lands, food
supplies, culture, and life itself, or blacks who remained, in
spite of all the rhetoric denouncing oppression, in chattel
slavery? There is no way that the American government
which came into power in the aftermath of the revolution
may be regarded as other than a regime privileging white,
male property-holders and as one victimizing in particular
the poor and propertyless, women, Indians, blacks. For all
of these human beings—not to mention George III and his

Tory adherents—political authority in the new nation must be deemed illegitimate. Notice, too, that there is no common ideological basis among such disparate interests, which may also be in conflict one with another; the regime is regarded as illegitimate because it treats each of these as victim in one way or another. In history, in fact, there is no political authority which can, categorically, be named legitimate and, depending upon how a given institution or person or class of persons may be situated any political authority will be seen to be legitimate and illegitimate coincidentally.

The factor of order provided by political authority can be considered in a parallel manner. For the British crown, the rebellion in the colonies meant the overthrow of order. For chattel slaves, the new government represented no more than an exchange of tyrannies in which the only order for blacks is oppression. For American Indians, the revolutionary victory portended chaos—further invasions and aggressions, seizures and occupations, war and genocide. For most women, the regime instituted offered not order but coerced servitude or treatment appropriate to mindless manikins. For the dispossessed, there was the anarchy of poverty and indebtedness and exclusion from the political process which ruled their existence. In short, the "order" provided by the ruling powers was that which enforced the vested interests of the incumbent rulers, and that meant disorder for those not rulers, whether they were principalities or persons.

Yet if the radically ecumenical outreach of Christ's intercession for the life of creation authorizes the church of Christ to live in advocacy in the world on behalf of all sorts and conditions of humanity, and this specifically so as they be victims of predatory political authority, then the church occurs at the interstices of political tumult and controversy. If the church is called to advocacy, in a biblical sense, as a way of expressing its imminent eschatological insight, then the church cannot withdraw or retreat or escape from political involvement; it cannot indulge equivocation or apathy or indifference. On the contrary, in freedom to take the part of any victim, the church is plunged into the most radical sort of political witness in which the church besets political authority on every side, incessantly, resiliently, eclectically, dynamically, and with the marvelous versatility which the diversity of the gifts of the Holy Spirit abundantly supplies. If in the witness of advocacy there be circumstances where the church, or some members of the body of the church, be found supporting incumbent political authority, that is a matter of temporary gratuity and not of stupid allegiance to secular thrones.

More commonly, as it appears to me, the church, or the people of the church, in intercession for multifarious victims of political authority are found in protest and opposition to the powers that be. Still, it must not be overlooked that resistance to a regime may be the recourse appropriate to recalling political authority to its vocation. To love the enemy or to bless those who persecute does not preclude political resistance or dissent where the enemy is the state or the system or an emperor or president. I have mentioned, earlier, how just such a witness was involved in the protests against the criminality of the prosecution of the war in Vietnam. The political resistance, then was, in part, an effort to seek the restoration of lawful and constitutional government. Sometimes more was involved. I remember, vividly, participating, on the evening before the second inauguration of Richard Nixon, in public worship, where the open intention focused upon the president and his captivations with arbitrary power and interminable war. When my turn came to speak that night, I invoked one of the church's ancient prayers of exorcism on behalf of Richard Nixon, then discernably possessed by the power of death in these definite ways. The intercession was for the restoration of *his* humanity: for his release: for his healing. I did this, if with some trepidation, though, I trust, also with due humility, because the crisis for the nation had exceeded official crime and unconstitutionality, as far as I understood, and at that point also involved how this person—the emperor himself—had become victim—perchance the most pathetic and dehumanized victim of all in the whole ordeal of America signified by the Vietnam war. So I said this prayer, which originated in the church's experience in such matters long ago, on behalf of the humanity of Mr. Nixon. The congregation, about a thousand were present, returned "Amen!" and then, again "Amen!" and, then, as if to make it perfectly clear that the prayer was *their* own prayer, they all stood and the "Amen!" was transposed into a thunderous ovation. "Bless those who persecute you; bless and do not curse them" (Rom. 12:14). That measures the outreach of the advocacy of the biblical witness.

The Nationhood of the Church

When and where the church participates in the biblical witness in history and is an advocate for any victim of political authority—or for a victim in any other sense of the power of death at work in the world—the church risks the suffering of the victim. That is enough to show the connection in the present age between the mission of the church and any persecution, ridicule or other hostility which the church endures. That is to say, in antagonistic circumstances, the church suffers as a surrogate for the world, bearing the burden of the victim and, for that matter, of the aggressor as well.

There is, unfortunately, a pathetic legacy of dissembling about this situation of the church. A familiar asspect of it is the romanticizing of the era of Roman persecution of the early church which, in effect, laments the closing of arena spectacles pitting lions against Christians as a way of excusing the corruption and floundering of the church ever since. The inference seems to be that the church should seek persecution in order to engender incentive to be stalwart in the gospel. Such sentiments are, of course, plainly refuted in the New Testament both by the accounts of the ministry of Jesus—there is no evidence that he sought crucifixion—and by the witness of the apostolic church—the indication is the apostles were very concerned to spare the church persecution. (See the First Letter of Peter.)

The church, anyway, needs no compulsion to gain persecution, in any circumstances at any time in this age, because the power of death, incarnate in the political principalities, as in other ways, is truly incorrigible. Death is the aggressor and though the apparitions and forms which the power of death assumes are variegated, that does not imply that death can be quantified. It is no longer the custom to cast Christians into dens of beasts, but that does not mean the persecution has ended. And, whatever else may be attributed to the impress of the Constantinian arrangement, its comity did not abate the hostility which the church, where it is exemplar and advocate of life, endures for the time being in this world.

In quite the same vein, too much is made of the witness of particular Christians so that it is regarded as exceptional (rather than exemplary) and so some few are installed as martyrs, as heroic figures, as super-Christians. An instance is found in the lore which has accrued to Dietrich Bonhoeffer. I do not hesitate at all to venture that Bonhoeffer would be deeply provoked by the way his witness has been construed as so unusual that it is unedifying to ordinary people of the church, so bold that it excuses inaction rather than inspiring it. Another case in point, within my direct knowledge, occurred when Daniel Berrigan, S.J., was seized by the federal police at my Block Island home while he was a fugitive felon, having resisted the criminal war policy of the incumbent regime in America. In covering the event, one of the Providence television stations interviewed John McLaughlin, who then was a Jesuit and a candidate for the United States Senate from Rhode Island, and who was later compensated for his defeat in that campaign by appointment to the White House staff where, in due course, he became the official Watergate casuist. In the television interview on August 11, 1970, McLaughlin was asked his reaction to the activities of his Jesuit brother. He rambled on for awhile about how some work for change from within the system (e.g. McLaughlin as senatorial candidate) while others act outside the system (e.g. Berrigan as convicted war resister). But, then, concluding, McLaughlin declared: "Of course, you must realize Dan is a *poet!*" He might have said "martyr" or "kook" or "prophet" or "lunatic" or "hero" or "fanatic" or "fool"—the intent was the same: to discharge Berrigan from the realm of common human beings and to dismiss Berrigan's witness by styling it exceptional.

The point is, of course, that there are no martyrs at all in the church because of the veracity of the sacrifice of the Word of God in Christ for the world. There is nothing to be added to Christ's sacrifice. No Christian in witness to Christ's sacrifice volunteers any sacrifice of his or her own. The whole idea of there being any martyrs for the gospel is an embellishment misleading the church and its members and furnishing pretext to simply cop-out.

This whole syndrome in the contemporary church sponsors the notion that, though there may be occasional poets, fools, or super-Christians, with the alleged ending of persecution, all that remains between the church and political authority are some few issues which may prompt intermittent incidents of individual civil disobedience. There are still some Quakers on the scene, plus scattered Anabaptists, but, in general, in the contemporary church, in America and places like America, the questions of obedience and conscience are usually deemed to affect individuals, not the church as an institution and society. And the decisions such persons make are thought to be idiosyncratic and, moreover, arrogant—that is, implicating a claim of superior insight into the will and judgment of God.

The term conscience is used only rarely in the New Testament, and not as such in the Old Testament. Apart from its use in association with obedience in ROMANS, where Paul makes no equation between conscience and the will of God, but, on the contrary, makes clear that conscience is subject to judgment, the most notable mention of conscience is in the First Epistle of Peter. That epistle expounds the meaning of baptism as the sacrament of the new and mature humanity of persons in Christ, of the new citizenship in Christ compared to the old citizenship under Caesar. Far from having eccentric denotations, conscience is an expression of the identification of baptized people with the whole of humanity.

Similarly, ROMANS 12 hinges the chapter's discourse on the life of the body of Christ in the world upon not being conformed to the world but being transformed by the renewal of the mind. In Christian faith, conscience does not mean a private, unilateral, self-serving, morally superior opinion held by an individual disconnected from the community, but it bespeaks the freedom to transcend self, to expend life, to share in suffering, to risk death for the sake of others and on behalf of the world which is integral to becoming a member of the corpus of the church. Conscience, for Christians, rather than being solitary or eccentric, bespeaks the church's witness of advocacy.

Let it be said that when I name the church, I do not have in mind some idealized church, or some disembodied or uninstitutionalized church, or just an aggregate of individuals. I mean the church in history, the church constituted and precedented in history at Pentecost, the church which is an organic reality: visible as a community, institutionalized as a society. I refer to the church as a new household or to the church as congregation. Most concretely, I name the church as the holy nation.

The church which is the holy nation is not metaphorical, but it is the church called into being at Pentecost: the church which is the new Israel of God in the world; the church which is both progeny of the biblical tradition of Zion and pioneer of the kingdom of God; the church which is the exemplary nation juxtaposed to all the other nations; the church which as a principality and institution transcends the bondage to death in the midst of fallen creation; the church which presents and represents in its corporate life creation restored in celebration of the Word of God; the church in which the vocation of worship and advocacy signifies the renewed vocation of every creature; the church which anticipates the imminent and prompt redemption of all of life.

The church's calling as the holy nation has been profoundly distorted since Pentecost, and, manifestly, especially so under the aegis of the Constantinian détente with the rulers and regimes of the present age. Insofar as there was in the fourth century definite incentive to enter that comity in order to alleviate persecution, the purpose remains unaccomplished. If Christians have been spared the savagery of beasts or if the more notorious vulgarities of emperor worship have been abated, other forms of persecution have succeeded and the hostility of demonic principalities and powers toward the church has not diminished. By the twentieth century, the enmity of the power of death toward the church had come to be enacted in the grandiose idolatry of the destiny of British colonial imperialism, or in the brutal devastation of the church following upon the Soviet Revolution, or in the ruthless Nazi usurpation of the church in the name of "Germanizing" or "purifying" Christianity so as to have this accomplice in the pursuit and in the incineration of the Jews.

Meanwhile, in America, the pluralism of religions and the multiplicity of denominations have abetted the inception of civil religion, which has assorted versions, but the major thrust of which imputes a unique moral status to the nation, a divine endorsement for America, which, in its most radical composition, disappropriates the vocation of church as the holy nation.

Thus the church becomes confined, for the most part, to the sanctuary, and is assigned to either political silence or to banal acquiescence. Political authority in America has sanctioned this accommodation principally by the economic rewards it bestows upon the church. The tax privilege, for example, to which the church has acceded, has been a practically conclusive inhibition to the church's political intervention save where it consists of applause for the nation's cause. Furthermore, the tax preference or political subsidy the church has so long received has enabled, perhaps more than anything else, the accrual of enormous, if unseemly, wealth. In the American comity, the church has gained so huge a propertied interest that its existence has become overwhelmingly committed to the management of property and the maintenance of the ecclesiastical fabric which that property affords. It is a sign certainly of the demonic in institutional life where the survival of the principality is the dominant morality. That mark is evident in very many professed churches in Amer-

ica. I cannot imagine any other way, at this point, to free
the church to recover its vocation as the exemplary principality or holy nation, than by notorious acts of disavowal
of this traffic with political authority. The church in America needs to divest property, not hoard it any longer and,
as part of that I urge renunciation of the tax privilege so
that the church could be freed to practice tax resistance.
If that portends direct collision with political authority
and involves such risks as official confiscation of church
properties—which it does—then my only response is that
it promises a way of consolidating losses.

The suppression of the comprehension of the church as
the holy nation or as the priest among the nations, whether
in America or elsewhere, causes, I think, the importance of
the dispersion of the church to be minimized or even overlooked. Yet it is impossible to contemplate the nationhood
of the church without retaining the sense of the eschatological imminence that has been previously discussed. The
imminence is conveyed where the church lives in dispersion
throughout the world, confronting every nation and tribe,
tongue and culture as an embassy of the Kingdom. Such
dispersion is, on one hand, incompatible with the Constantinian ethos, but, on the other, it verifies the truly ecumenical reality of the church in this world.

More than that, the dispersion inherent in the church's
identity as the priest of nations and forerunner of the Kingdom is, I believe, temporal as much as spatial. The church
is dispersed in space and thus indulges no dependency upon
particular nations or regimes of nations but by its presence
disrupts every nation and every regime. The church also
remains dispersed in time, forebearing to become vested in
a specific institutional mode indefinitely, or as if in per-
petuity, but the event of the church constantly, repeatedly
fractures time. That is to say, the church as institution or
nation is, first of all, an event of the moment, gathered
here or there, but that does not predetermine whether or
how the church will appear again. The church is episodic in
history; the church lives in imminence so that the church
has no permanent locale or organization which predicates

its authenticity as the church. This may seem a hectic doctrine of the church to the Constantinian mentality. It is. But it is so because it suggests the necessity of breaking away from Constantinian indoctrination in order to affirm the poise of the church awaiting the second advent of Jesus Christ.

epilogue

Bless those who persecute you; bless and do not curse them.

Romans 12:14

Also (the beast) was allowed to make war on the saints and to conquer them.

Revelation 13:7

A Homily
on the Significance
of the Defeat
of the Saints

A most obstinate misconception associated with the gospel of Jesus Christ is that the gospel is welcome in this world. The conviction—endemic among churchfolk—persists that, if problems of misapprehension and misrepresentation are overcome and the gospel can be heard in its own integrity, the gospel will be found attractive by people, become popular and, even, be a success of some sort.

This idea is both curious and ironical because it is bluntly contradicted in Scripture, and in the experience of the continuing biblical witness in history from the event of Pentecost unto the present moment. There is no necessity to cite King Herod or Judas Iscariot or any notorious enemies of the gospel in this connection; after all, while Christ was with them, no one in his family and not a single one of the disciples accepted him, believed his vocation or loved his gospel.

After Pentecost, where the Acts of the Apostles evince an understanding and the confession of the gospel, resistance and strife concerning the gospel are equally in evidence among the pioneer Christians, while the consternation and hostility of the world for the gospel was very agitated and quickly aggressive. Furthermore, the Letters of the New Testament betell congregations nurtured in the faith amidst relentless temptations of apostasy and confusion and conformity.

Subsequent events in the life of the church, especially

since the inception of Christendom in the Constantinian Arrangement, and with the institutional sophistication of the churches, only modify this situation by complicating it. There is, simply, no reason to presuppose that *anyone* will find the gospel, as such, likable.

The categories of popularity or progress or effectiveness or success are impertinent to the gospel. That has been implicit, here, in the effort throughout this book to deal simultaneously (rather than separately) and confessionally (instead of academically) with the passages about political authority in ROMANS and in REVELATION. The matter is signified forcefully in the introit to ROMANS 13 by the text, "Bless those who persecute you, bless and do not curse them" (Rom. 12:14). As has been mentioned, this is no adage prompted by sentimentality. It is a statement of the extraordinary relationship between Christians and the ruling principalities radically constituted in the discernment of the imminence of the judgment of the Word of God in history by which Christians are authorized to recall political authority to the vocation of worship and reclaim dominion over creation for humanity. It is a statement about the implication of the Lordship of Jesus Christ for the rulers of this age. To bless the powers that be, in the midst of persecution, exposes and confounds their blasphemous status more cogently and more fearlessly than a curse.

In the Book of Revelation, the issue is expressed more severely and more straightforwardly than perhaps anywhere in the Bible. "Also [the beast] was allowed to make war on the saints and to conquer them" (Rev. 13:7). On the face of it, this is not an appealing or popular text. That may in itself be an explanation of why it has been so often ignored or even suppressed by commentators or why it has seldom been mentioned, much less commended, by preachers. I have read it, it seems, a thousand times, and I admit that I am tempted to wish it were not there or to locate some pretext to dismiss it or gainsay it. I find no way to rationalize the verse away. Unlike some other passages in REVELATION, it does not afford evasion or oversight because it is esoteric or enigmatic. It is a most unambiguous and matter-of-fact statement. It says what it says: during the present age, the Word of God allows predacious ruling authority to wage war on the Christians and to defeat them.

For the time being, in the era of the fall, until the consummation of this history in the judgment of the Word of God, the beast knows success and indulges victory; the saints suffer aggression and know defeat. Surely the text mocks every effort, undertaken in the name of the Christian witness in this world, which is informed by calculations about effectiveness, progress, approval, acclaim—or any of the varieties of success. And that not only in circumstances where the church openly imitates or emulates the way of the beast, but also where the calculation prior to action or program is more guileful or pretentious and claims foreknowledge of how the matter will be judged by the Word of God. The churches and, within them, both social activists and private pietists, are virtually incorrigible—despite the admonition of REVELATION 13:7—in practicing some such deliberation before risking any putative witness. Where that be the situation, the professed saints succumb to the power of death by their profound doubt in the efficacy of the resurrection and by their direct dispute of the activity of judgment in the Word of God. So they—attempting vainly to forestall or obviate defeat—are defeated anyway, ignominiously.

REVELATION 13:7 contains no melancholy message. It authorizes hope for the saints—and, through their vocation of advocacy, hope for the whole of creation—which is grounded in realistic expectations concerning this present age, enabling the church—as the first beneficiary of the resurrection—to confront the full and awesome militancy of the power of death incarnate in the ruling principalities, and otherwise, in this world, nourishing patience for the judgment of the Word of God and, meanwhile, trusting nothing else at all. This seemingly troublesome text about the defeat of the saints by the beast is, preeminently, a reference to the accessibility of the grace of the Word of God for living now. To mention the defeat of the saints means to know the abundance of grace. And that prompts no rejection of or withdrawal from the world as it is, but, on the contrary, the most fearless and resilient involvement in this world.

Since the rubrics of success or power or similar gain are impertinent to the gospel, the witness of the saints looks foolish where it is most exemplary. One American political prisoner—Philip Berrigan—addressed that characterization of the defeat of the saints when he was sentenced upon conviction for attempting to dig a grave on the lawn of the White House in rebuke of the rule of the beast:

> In pondering a few words for this occasion, I happened on Paul's First Letter to the Church at Corinth. . . . "We are fools on Christ's account" (1 Cor. 4:10). In a modest fashion, I have sought membership in this company of fools. . . . Through over 39 months in prison, through long fasts and bouts of solitary confinement, through two indictments while in jail, I have been reckoned a fool, by pharaohs and friends alike. . . .
>
> Let no one find our foolishness puzzling. It is as simple as honoring the 5th commandment, and rejecting official legitimations of murder. It is obedience to the truth and compassion of Christ; or recognizing no enemy in the world. . . . It is as simple as respecting the planet as common property, as common gift and heritage. That is the idiot vision—that is the summons and task. For that, as Paul promised, one risks becoming the world's refuse, the scum of all (1 Cor. 4:13). . . . [T]he fools will never abandon hope, nor cease to live it.

This foolishness of the saints, this witness in the midst of defeat, is wrought in the relationship of justification and judgment, in which one who knows justification to be a gift of the Word of God is spared no aggression of the power of death but concedes no tribute to the power of death while awaiting the vindication of the Word of God in the coming of Jesus Christ in judgment.